About the Author

Caroline lives in rural Hampshire, UK with Mr. Dragon Lady and their dogs Molly and Treacle. She initially met dragons and their energy in 2002 but really started to work with them in 2005. The last 17 years have taught Caroline even more about the power and purpose behind dragons, allowing her to become the UK's leading Dragon Lady, author and channeller. She enjoys enlightening and sharing dragon wisdom with thousands of people globally and in 2020 she released *Dragon Path Oracle Cards*. Based at Dragon HQ she continues to concentrate on working with the dragon realms, channelling and teaching with these powerful, magnificent beings of change.

How to Live with Dragons

The Dragon Path Guide to Healing,
Empowerment and Adventure

Caroline Mitchell

WATKINS

Sharing Wisdom Since 1893

How to Live with Dragons
Caroline Mitchell

This edition first published in the UK and USA
in 2022 by Watkins, an imprint of Watkins Media Limited
Unit 11, Shepperton House, 89–93 Shepperton Road
London N1 3DF

enquiries@watkinspublishing.com

1 2 3 4 5 6 7 8 9 10

Typeset by Lapiz

Printed and bound in the UK by TJ Books Ltd

A CIP record for this book is available from the British Library

ISBN: 978-1-78678-699-9 (Hardback)
ISBN: 978-1-78678-705-7 (eBook)

www.watkinspublishing.com

Contents

The Preamble

Welcome to the world of *How to Live with Dragons*. If this book has found its way into your hands, there is a pretty good chance that you have already encountered the dragon realms and are wondering: "What on earth is going on?" and/or "What do I do now?"

The writing of this book has taken an age. I made numerous attempts at creating the content – what to include, what to leave out, how to get across what living with dragons is really like and how to go about it. I also had to consider whether to include what dragons are, why they are here and how you, the reader, can enhance your connection to them.

While pulling this all together, I tried to follow some form of start to finish guide. But this was becoming too dry and dull. I tried to make it linear, following some kind of sequence that would make sense to you, the reader, rather than my somewhat haphazard introduction and learning from dragons. But that did not work either.

So, instead, here you have what the dragons have given me, as it feels right. Rather than a sequential journey, this book is a series of chapters that you can dip in and out of as and when you feel you need to.

You can of course read the book from cover to cover, and I will try to put it into some kind of order for you, until the dragons say otherwise.

My Dragon Encounters

My journey with the dragons over two decades has been remarkable and unremarkable in equal measure. There were times when I doubted my sanity and my natural abilities. My journey has been full of pitfalls and mines, euphoria and excitement, and more than one temper tantrum, from me rather than the dragons! Self-doubt and self-flagellation have been a part of that journey too. I didn't know of anyone else doing what I was doing with dragons, so there was no one to bounce ideas off or compare notes with.

In many respects it has been and continues to be a lonely path to tread.

As humans we all believe we gain our validation from another source, from our outside world. We all crave it, to give us confidence and to boost our self-belief. We think we need others to believe in us before we can believe in ourselves; that this validation must come from another person, a peer group and so on. For when another human believes in us, we then begin to believe in ourselves and learn to trust ourselves too.

The dragons have taught me that this does not need to be the case.

When I began my dragon journey it was the height of the Angelic Season (the dragons' words, not mine). The dragons have historically been depicted as bad-tempered fire-breathing, maiden-stealing, gold-hoarding beasts of our folklore, fairy tales and legends. So in a nutshell, unpleasant beasts to be around. Yet here I was, gradually bringing these beings into my life. Despite wondering if it was a wise thing to do, I felt compelled to keep going, to follow the path they laid out for me.

It has been quite a journey to date, one that is continuously unfolding, for they and I are constantly growing together.

Here I share my knowledge and that of the dragons. Some of this is from the knowledge they have given to me, and other parts will be what they have taught me.

As I have been writing, rewriting, perusing and wondering about the content of this book, the form it would take and the message it would impart to whoever finds it in their hands, I came to realize a few things about the process, and this made me question the dragons about it more deeply.

This book and the work within it is a journey of self-discovery for you, dear reader, as you embark upon your dragon life. It is an exploration of the self, of healing, of often deeply held beliefs and, on occasions, of emotional pain.

Our wish (mine and the dragons) is that within its pages you find your uniqueness, your quirkiness, your passion, your power and your truth. Our wish is that you are able to embrace it all, along with a deepening spiritual understanding and relationship with your dragon kin.

Once these first foundations have been laid, healing can take place, with liberation within your reach. From this grounded point you can fly high with your winged family.

So now I welcome you aboard. And advise you to grab your hat and hold on tight – your journey with the dragons may become a little bumpy at times. But hopefully you will also enjoy the ride!

Why Dragons?

I have wondered "why dragons?" *a lot* over the years.

The answer I received from my dragon guide Solomon was: "We dragons are part of your spiritual evolution, both as a species and as a planet."

Ultimately dragons are here to support our life path during this incarnation, wherever that journey may take us. They are not averse to doing the heavy lifting that is often required on our planet. They know that life is not all love and light, no matter how much we would like it to be. They are here to guide us all along our chosen path, to deal with what life throws at us, to pick us up if we fall and teach us we can when we believe we can't.

As the spiritual warriors of Earth, their gifts to us are healing, empowerment, integrity, authenticity and deeper spiritual understanding.

Dragon Clans

Any group of dragons is known as a "clan".

Within my Dragon Path Oracle deck I have included four clans. So if you are familiar with the deck you will already know the Earth Walks, Galactics, Grand Masters and Guardians. Other dragons and clans that I have come to know are the Helix Ray Dragons, Magdalene's Sapphire Dragons, Dragons of Light, Dragons of the Land and Earth Dragons.

All of these are covered in more detail throughout the book. There are undoubtedly others too, which you will encounter through your own dragon work.

In essence the dragons loosely work with the format below.

Healing Dragons

Personal healing, personal responsibility and accountability is the first lesson that the dragons teach and show us. They teach about shadow self, spiritual bypassing and being present. This leads us to personal truth, owning who we are and personal power.

The dragons' view is that we can't hold the vibration and frequency of the work to be done on Earth if we let fears, doubts, old patterning and wounds stand in our way. If we believe that lack of self-belief or lack of confidence, anger, jealousy, bitterness or resentment is our lot in life, if we do not push and work through self-limiting beliefs and self-imposed restrictions, we strangle off our chance to grow, heal, develop and more.

When we feel we are voiceless, powerless, when we are not heard, we are completely unable to stand in our truth or in the awesome power of the amazing beings we truly are.

The dragons ask that we start the process by being brutally honest with ourselves.

Do not fall into the trap of false modesty or believing that someone else is better than you or that everything is your fault. It is not for you to carry the blame for others' actions or behaviours. Nor can you bypass or ignore your shortcomings; you are, after all, human.

Nor will the dragons allow you to project or blame. They request that you face your fears, negativity, self-doubt and more. This is possibly their biggest teaching and can be a tough path to traverse, but the dragons will guide you if you listen. And sometimes you have to hear with your eyes or see with your ears. And no, these are not typos – these are deliberate.

Each and every one of you is an amazingly awesome human being.

You will notice as you work with your dragons that they are incredibly direct but will guide you well and true if you allow them. Let them take you by the hand as they guide you forward, toward freedom, laughter, empowerment, self-belief and above all else honouring yourself as the valuable and worthwhile divine being you are.

We more or less ignored the angels and the gentler messages they had and continue to have for us. We carried on regardless, ignoring their quiet nudges to heal and grow.

The dragons are not here to stroke your feathers and pander to your self-illusion, self-delusion or ego. Nor is it their role to make you feel good about yourself unless you truly need it. Instead they are here to guide you, get you on your feet, take action, heal and be the change we wish to see in your world.

They urge you to be a guide and light for others to follow. To heal and show the world what a remarkable, beautiful human being you are. Yes, I dare say, _you_. Like us all you will continue to be a work in progress, but now you know who you are and you are working on it.

Dragons of the Land

These guys connect to the Earth's energy lines (matrix lines (for more details, see chapter 14) and not necessarily ley lines), although they do connect to sacred sites and the eight festivals – for more details on festivals, see chapter 10. The dragons frequently communicate with us through nature, so they teach us to listen, stop and take notice.

Dragons guide us to connect to the energy of the land, so there are those which are Shamanic in nature. They also encourage us to repair the Earth's matrix, as this has become distorted and out of whack. If we are to thrive, the Earth's energies require care and rebalancing.

We need to learn to work together as a species rather than be in competition with one another or to be better than anything or anyone else.

This sounds all very utopian I know, but that is their message.

High Vibrational Dragons

This group combines all the other work, plus connecting all the matrixes of Earth, the star systems and the crystalline structures in the Earth.

The dragons then take us into a journey of body light coding, DNA upgrades and DNA recoding.

All of this tunes us into and aligns us with our light body, *Merkabah*, alignment of our personal matrix and our connection to each other, the planet, the galaxies and the Universe.

Added to this are the new chakra colours and frequency. From there we are able to work in the various dimensions from fourth dimension to at least seventh dimension, if not beyond.

Here we are also introduced to the Mary Magdalene's Sapphire Ray Dragon, the Dragons of Light and the Helix Ray Dragons.

Other Things to Consider

Before embarking upon this journey fully you need to ask yourself these two questions: Are you ready to do the work with the dragons? Are you ready to be the change you wish to see in the world around you?

If so, welcome aboard!

You may like to treat yourself to a new notebook or journal specifically for your dragon writings and discoveries. There is a section on journaling with the dragons in chapter six.

At various points in this book you may like to enlist the help of a friend when you practice the meditations. Doing it this way means that one of you reads the meditation aloud while the other one meditates, and then you swap places. Or you may prefer to record your meditations so that you can listen to them whenever it suits you and as frequently as you would like to.

You may wish to set up a particular space within your home or garden just for your work with the dragons. This is not essential but it does help you to settle more quickly into your work and leave the stresses of the day behind.

DRAGON TALK

Before we begin, the dragons have this message for you:

"*To do dragon you need to go within,
nothing with dragon is outside of you. You
are the Universe, it is within you. You have
that connection, it is there.*

"*Go inwards always, connect with the
soup of the Universe, the sea of energy,
everything, every molecule is the Universe
and all the knowledge is held within it.
All you need to do is tap in and listen,
it is all there.*"

Are you ready to work with and meet your dragons?

Part
One

LIVE WITH DRAGONS

So your dragon journey begins.

In part one I endeavour to give you the grounding and tools required to connect with your personal dragons. This will empower you to activate your dragon journey and build a friendship that will last beyond this lifetime.

Here I discuss energy, colour, protection and receiving a chakra and energetic upgrade from the dragons, among other topics. The dragons will take you on a journey to the great temple of Atlantis and more. It's quite an adventure!

CHAPTER

1

Preparing for the Dragons

When I first encountered the dragons' energy fully in the mid 2000s, their energy could be overwhelming and left me feeling off balance, sometimes for a few days. Here I endeavour to show you techniques so that you do not have to flounder about in the dark. These lessons taught me a great deal about dragon energy and how not to do it! My hope here is to give you a good solid grounding and share with you how to get the most from your dragon encounters.

But first the dragons want me to give you some context and background information.

About Dragons

The dragons have been around since the beginning of time. They tell me that some dragons helped to create the Universe and everything within it, including Earth, the galaxies and all the dimensions. Dragons are wholly energetic beings now, although some have had a physical existence here on Earth. I do wonder if this was back in the age of the dinosaurs or before, as though they were keeping an eye on what they helped to create.

From an energy perspective, dragons are quite different from our usual spirit guides and the angelic realms, but that does not mean that they do not work with the other realms to support and guide us.

Many of you will be familiar with angel energy, its lightness for instance, or your spirit guides, which all carry their own unique vibration. The dragons too have their own vibration; it is actually a frequency rather than a vibration. This frequency can knock you off balance and leave you feeling somewhat ungrounded. Since the dragons are powerful and huge, in both stature and energy, their frequency allows them to carry a deeper and more powerful energy.

Dragons have a penchant for colour, sacred geometry, sounds and symbols. This is all frequency and makes up the very fabric of our Universe. Each of these topics can be studied as a standalone subject if they pique your interest.

Connecting with Dragons

I am often asked: "How do I connect with my dragons?" and "How can I improve my connection with them?" The short answer is meditation. Get to know your dragons' energy and vibration and how they work and communicate with you. I will cover all of this and more in the coming pages.

Dragons have been cropping up unbidden for a few years, especially over the last five years or so as they hit our collective consciousness, and it is really not uncommon for them to suddenly appear to you in meditation. I receive a lot of questions from people asking if what they are experiencing is real and what they should do about or with the dragon that has appeared unbidden and so on. Connecting with dragons can feel a little overwhelming at times. But remember that it is more than likely that the dragon has chosen you rather than you consciously seeking out the dragon.

Frequently when you first encounter dragons they will have two colours: one colour running from under their chin down their throats, under their tummies to the tip of their tail, and another colour running across the top.

Many people worry when they first encounter their dragons that they can't see them nor hear them. Again this is not uncommon.

So let us address these two particular issues.

Dragons are huge (for the most part anyway) beings of light. When I first encountered them I saw them simply as distant silhouettes overhead, and after that hardly saw them at all, which again is really common. People often say that they have a sense of their dragon yet can't see them. Seriously do not worry about it, as it all depends on your sentient abilities and where your strengths lie. It is these abilities and strengths that the dragons will work with.

Others say they see a dragon's eye really close up, or scales, but rarely the full image of their dragon. Again this is not unusual, so do not get caught up in it, worrying you are doing it wrong. The dragons love to use these situations as lessons – to them every day is a school day.

If you have honed clairvoyant abilities there is a good chance you will see your dragon in all their magnificence. But if you do not, your other "clairs" will come into play, such as clairaudience, clairsentience and claircognisence. If you are not familiar with the clairs, here is a quick overview.

- ⫸ Clairvoyance (clear seeing) is the ability to see spirits or energy.
- ⫸ Clairaudience (clear hearing) is the ability to hear words, phrases or music from spirit.
- ⫸ Clairsalience (clear smelling) is the ability to smell something out of the ordinary (such as your grandpa's pipe or your mum's perfume) so you associate a smell with anyone who is in the spirit realm.

➤ Clairsentience (clear sensing) is the ability to sense or feel spirits and energy – often this can be picking up someone's emotion, illness or pain from the spirit world.

➤ Claircognisence (clear knowing) is one of the hardest senses of all the clairs to work with as you simply just know stuff and you have no idea how or why you should know it, but you also know it is right!

Picking up on the clairaudience, do not be surprised if you do not hear your dragon to start with. Dragons do not have any kind of formal spoken language as we understand it. They are much more telepathic, which is why they seem to work well with people who have a stronger sense of claircognisence. It is rare to actually hear your dragon speak, but if you do you will notice the language they use is often direct and straightforward, using clipped short sentences. Over the years they have become much better at communicating with us for they are extremely talented beings and nothing is unsurmountable for them.

Dragons like to keep things simple, straightforward and clear. They are heart-based creatures, which means everything they do is from the heart. In other words you also need to get out of your head and into your heart; you can't "think" dragon – you have to "feel" dragon. Working with the dragons is a partnership and collaboration, a joining of heart and soul.

When you are heart centred, you tend to be naturally more present and grounded. The dragons frequently talk about us humans as being in our heads too much, and how out of step we are as a species with the natural world. If you spend a lot of time on your electronic devices (which takes you away from being present and heart based), be aware that you will be in line for a "dragon slap".

It is much easier to connect with the dragons if you are mindful, heart centred, grounded and present. The dragons tell me that this means you are finally listening, have got out of your head and can actually hear them over your constant cacophony of mind chatter.

There is knock on effect to all this – when you are being more present you have a greater understanding of yourself and your emotions and you have a far greater self-awareness. This is one of the dragons' greatest teachings – awareness of self.

If you are familiar with yoga, tai chi or mindfulness, you will be familiar with being present and connecting with the breath so you should find the following exercise relatively straightforward.

Head and Heart Meditation

Note: It is good practice to keep a written record of all your experiences. You will be amazed at the insights you have gained and your progress when you look back on it.

1. Find your comfortable seated position and gently close your eyes.
2. Roll your shoulders backwards and down a few times. Then slowly roll your head first one way then the other, in full circles, three or four times, stretching your neck as far as you comfortably can. Be aware of any tightness or tension. Do not force it; enjoy the movement and the stretch.
3. Bring your head back to centre to its usual position and drop your chin very slightly so the bones in your neck are in a complete straight line with the rest of your spine. Keep your shoulders drawn gently back and down.
4. Keeping your eyes gently closed, become aware of your breathing. Begin by taking three or four deep, slow breaths in. As you breathe in gently blow your

tummy out, a little like blowing up a balloon in your belly. Allow your breath to return to its natural rhythm. You may feel a little light headed after the deeper breathing if you are a shallow, chest breather.

5. Take your focus and full attention to your nose (maybe your nostrils or the tip of your nose). You may like to follow your breath in as far as you can, maybe to your throat or chest before exhaling. Allow a natural flow of in and out breaths, maintaining your attention on each. You may notice the air feels cooler on the "in breath", while the exhale may feel warmer. If your mind begins to wander or thoughts start to bubble to the surface, simply bring your awareness and focus back to the breath. Stay with this focus for a few minutes, allowing mind and body to slow down, to calm and settle.

6. Once you have settled into the breath you take your focus inwards to your heart chakra. To do this, allow your heart chakra to expand with each breath. When you are ready allow your consciousness and awareness to start to drop toward your heart, going deeper and deeper and deeper with each breath. Allow a feeling of quiet calm to settle over you.

7. Stay with this until you feel ready to rejoin your physical life.

When you are ready, wiggle your fingers and toes, have a gentle stretch and softly open your eyes, allowing your vision and focus to return gently. Quietly do a mental check in with yourself to see how you feel. Try to remember to stay present with your body and mind in your normal waking state.

Once you are fully back, make sure you have a glass of water to hand and write up your experiences in your journal. Be as clear and as specific as you can be in your recollection. As you write, a deeper understanding and clarity will come to you. You may like to record things like how you felt, any colours or images you experienced or any emotions that surfaced for you.

As you go through this process you will gradually notice differences in how you feel. Your physical body and mind will feel much calmer and quieter. You will discover that if your energies and mind have felt scattered they will draw back to you and your energetic system will feel far more balanced. Your mind will be much clearer but more importantly you will be grounded and present. And this is the key for working with dragons. The deeper you ground, the higher you can fly with them.

There are another couple of techniques you may like to try out too. Here I guide you to get to know your own personal energy and introduce you to the extended chakra system. Over time you will find which meditations suit you the best. Practise with them all and see which ones you actually like. Remember that each day may be different so go with what feels right. This is the first lesson from the dragons: Follow what feels right to you.

Your Personal Energy Meditation

This may seem like a convoluted exercise when you first read through it. So I suggest you read it a couple of times to become familiar with the ideas behind it before giving it a go. Do not get caught up here with "Am I doing this right – it's got to be perfect" or other mind nonsense. The exercise is a guide for you to connect to your energy and get the feel of it; it is not set in stone.

You may find it helpful to enlist the help of a friend to read the meditation aloud for you. You can then swap places once one of you has completed the meditation until you are both comfortable and familiar with it.

You will notice here that the dragons will not let you rush things. This lesson is also about slowing everything down. The first meditation is a part of that process, so do not rush or be impatient with yourself. Give yourself the time you need to complete and explore it and to enjoy it.

1. Sit comfortably with your feet on the floor. Notice how your body feels – warm, cold, soft, hard. Be aware of all the sensations beneath your feet. Feel where the chair meets your legs and your back. Give this your full focus.
2. Slowly take a deep breath in and feel your belly starting to blow out and expand. This is like trying to blow up a balloon in your tummy. Slowly let the breath out and repeat twice more. Remember to breathe right down into your tummy as far as you can.
3. You may like to roll your head in full gentle circles, stretching out any tightness or kinks in your neck. Then roll your shoulders slowly and gently a few times, taking them right up to your ears and then dropping

then down and back. Repeat as many times as you feel necessary in both directions.

4. Allow your breathing to return to its natural rhythm. Take your attention and focus inwards, keeping your breathing regular. Get a sense of your body's rhythm and how it feels, and you will begin to get a sense of your own personal energy. This will most likely be in or around your solar plexus. Everyone experiences their personal energy differently. Try not to get tangled up in your thoughts as you observe your energy. Let the energy find its own path as it flows and moves through your body. Become aware of how the energy moves – is it slow and steady, trickling, rushing, does it stop and start?

5. Follow your energy flow through your tummy, down your legs, back up again, all the way up to your chest, through your organs, the layers of muscle, bone, tendons, all through your complete physical body. Follow the energy's journey down your arms to the tips of your fingers and back up again across your shoulders and up your neck into your head, all the time observing and not interfering with its journey.

6. Follow your energy flow through your chakras. Have an awareness of how it feels to you. Become aware of its colour or colours and follow this around your entire body once more.

7. Once you have established your energy colour, become aware of its texture – is it smooth, rough or wispy? There is no right or wrong to colours or textures; they are what they are. Some people observe their energy being like electricity; others have flowing lava, lace, silk, water or mist.

8. Once you have become accustomed to your energy and have a feel for it, gradually bring your awareness back to your normal waking conscious state.

When you are ready to come back to this world, wiggle your fingers and toes, have a gentle stretch and softly open your eyes, allowing your vision and focus to return gently. Quietly do a mental check in with yourself to see how you feel.

Once you are fully back make sure you have a glass of water to hand and write up your experiences in your journal. Be as clear and as specific as you can be in your recollection. As you write, a deeper understanding and clarity will come to you.

The Extended Chakra System Exercise

Now you are familiar with your personal energy, let us take it to the next level and explore the extended chakra system. Many people find being grounded and anchored a challenge so if you are serious about working with dragons you may find the following exercise incredibly useful.

In the following exercise you are going to build on the previous one of connecting to your personal energy. But now you will take it a step further by connecting deeply into the Earth through the Earth's chakras.

Below is the extended chakra system starting with the higher vibrational energy centre of the Interdimensional gateway all the way down to the heart of Mother Earth.

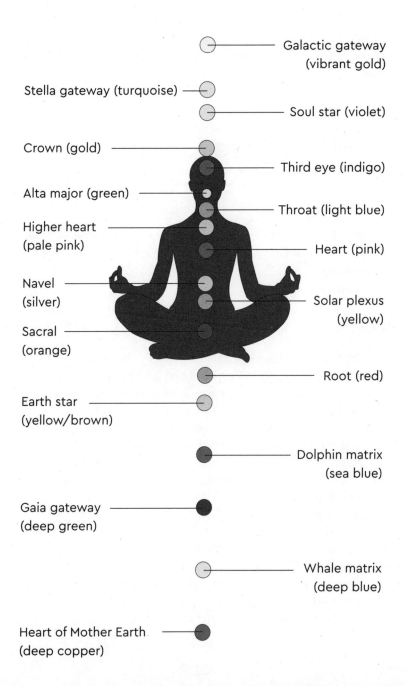

Interdimensional gateway
(bright white)

Galactic gateway
(vibrant gold)

Stella gateway (turquoise)

Soul star (violet)

Crown (gold)

Third eye (indigo)

Alta major (green)

Throat (light blue)

Higher heart
(pale pink)

Heart (pink)

Navel
(silver)

Solar plexus
(yellow)

Sacral
(orange)

Root (red)

Earth star
(yellow/brown)

Dolphin matrix
(sea blue)

Gaia gateway
(deep green)

Whale matrix
(deep blue)

Heart of Mother Earth
(deep copper)

You can use the following exercise to get to know each of the chakras, how they feel and what they mean to you. Try not to think it but be guided by your feelings and sensations as you connect to each one. And of course there is a good chance that your dragon will join you and add their three pen'th worth.

Deep Earth Meditation

I invite you to read through this mediation a couple of times and become familiar with it as there are three options. Decide before you begin which one you would like to do and how far you would like to go.

Leave yourself ample time to explore your meditation. The dragons encourage you to slow down and take your time.

1. Take a slow, deep breath in and feel your tummy starting to expand. Slowly let the breath out and repeat twice more. Remember to breathe right down into your tummy. Then allow your breathing to return to its natural rhythm with regular, steady breaths. Get a sense of your body's rhythm and how it feels to you.
2. Keeping your focus you will begin to get a sense of your own personal energy. Observe your energy (without getting tangled in your thoughts) as it flows and moves around and through your body. Avoid trying to guide it; just let it find its own path.
3. Follow the energy flow through your tummy, down your legs, back up again, all the way up to your chest, through your organs, the layers of muscle, bone, tendons, all through your complete physical body. Follow your energy's journey down your arms, to

the tips of your fingers back up again, across your shoulders, and up your neck into your head.

4. Take your energy through your chakras, being aware of how it feels and its colour or maybe colours. Is your energy the same as last time or has it changed in some way? Become aware of its texture.

5. Now focus on your energy so it begins to build in your root chakra. This is your first grounding chakra. Feel your energy gather in your root chakra, filling your entire pelvic area. When you are ready allow it to flow down your legs, out through your feet and through the floor and into the Earth. A little way into the Earth you will connect to your Earth star chakra, the first of the Earth centres. Feel the gentle tug of your energy as it connects and fills this chakra with your energy. Once this feels complete, take your focus down deeper. Connect to the dolphin matrix; feel the sense of lightness and joy here, where you are grounding and connecting more deeply with the Earth.

6. When you are ready, move your focus down, following your energy's journey. The journey may not be a straight line; it may meander and zigzag as your energy flows through the deeper Earth layers. Follow your energy deeper toward Gaia gate, which is the first anchor point for your energy. Spend some time with the energy and sensations of Gaia gate, locate your anchor point and loop your energy to a tether (anything from a crystal bed to a large rock). There are no rules; follow your intuition or your dragon's guidance, watching for what comes to mind and feels right.

Here you can continue your journey downwards or choose to return. It does not matter what you decide to do. To go back up, follow your energy flow back through the layers of the Earth to the dolphin matrix, up to your Earth star and back into your feet and up your legs to your root chakra. Open your eyes when you are ready to come back into this physical reality.

Alternatively you may continue your journey, grounding and anchoring more deeply. To continue downwards:

7. Follow your energy's journey taking you deeper and deeper downwards, following your energy flow until you connect with the whale matrix. Feel the ancientness of this chakra, all the wisdom held within it.

8. When you are ready continue your journey down further once more. Accompany your energy as it flows ever downwards to the heart of Mother Earth chakra. Connect here to feel her nurturing essence, holding your energy, anchoring and enfolding you. You may like to stay a while in this deeply nourishing energy to revitalize and calm your senses.

9. When you are ready, begin your journey back up toward your body. Flow to the whale matrix, connecting here once more. Moving on up to Gaia gate, checking in with your tether point, following the flow up to dolphin and then to your Earth star, finally following your energy back into your feet and up your legs to your root chakra.

You can finish your meditation here or you may like to continue and connect to the higher chakras. When you are ready to come back to this world, wiggle your fingers and toes, have a gentle stretch and softly open your eyes, allowing your vision and focus to return gently. Quietly do a mental check in with yourself to see how you feel.

Once you are fully back make sure you have a glass of water to hand and write up your experiences in your journal. Be as clear and as specific as you can be in your recollection. As you write, a deeper understanding and clarity will come to you.

If you would like to continue your energy journey and connect with the higher chakras, bring the energy up through the root, sacral, navel, solar plexus until it settles in the heart chakra.

10. High above you in the stratosphere, visualize a golden beam of light. Begin to draw the golden light down.
11. Draw the light down through your interdimensional gateway, down through your galactic gateway chakra, stella gateway, down through the soul star chakra, drawing it on down through the top of your head into your crown chakra, then in through your third eye, alta major, throat, higher heart to finally your heart.
12. Allow the energy to blend and flow through your body, giving yourself some time to adjust to this new energy frequency and vibration.
13. Spend a few minutes becoming accustomed to how you feel.

When you are ready to come back to this world, wiggle your fingers and toes, have a gentle stretch and softly open your eyes, allowing your vision and focus to return gently. Quietly do a mental check in with yourself to see how you feel.

Once you are fully back make sure you have a glass of water to hand and write up your experiences in your journal. Be as clear and as specific as you can be in your recollection. As you write, a deeper understanding and clarity will come to you.

When using this exercise you do not need to go through closing the Earth chakras or the higher 'out of body' chakras. These are always on tap, ready to receive and hold your energy. The only ones you "close down" are the ones around your body.

Closing the Chakras

As you are probably aware you can't close your chakras down, not fully anyway as they are a part of your life force, your life energy. What you can do is bring them down into what I think of as a "snooze state". In effect what you are doing is telling your energy system to have a rest – that its work is complete for now. It is a little like hanging up at the end of phone call.

This closing exercise is carried out at the end of all spiritual work you do, whether you are doing meditation, visualization or any form of spiritual readings or healings.

It is also good practice to have an energy cleansing routine at the end of any spiritual work you do, especially if you are working within the spiritual field all day, such as at a fair or psychic event. Remember to do an energy clearing visualization and close down at the end of the day.

There are a number of ways to disconnect from the dragons and spirit. This depends on how your mind works and how you visualize.

Closing Visualization

To close your chakras down, you always start at the crown chakra first. Doing it this way means you are disconnecting from the universal energies from your dragon and spirit guides.

1. Imagine each chakra has a light switch or cord attached to it. At your crown chakra, visualize a pull cord or a flick switch.
2. Flick the switch (or pull the cord) and visualize your crown chakra shrinking in size. See it becoming smaller and smaller. You can take it down to the size of an orange or pinprick of light. Follow what feels right to you.
3. Take your focus down to your third eye, repeating the process of shrinking the energy of the chakra. Move on down through your throat, heart, solar plexus, navel, sacral and root charkas in turn, taking each of them down to the size that feels right.

You can use and visualize any technique that works for you. I have had students using dimmer switches to turn their chakras down or visualizing a flower closing up into a tight bud.

Any positive energy that you do not require for yourself can be released into the Earth through the soles of your feet.

Dragons and Protection

I have found that one of the quickest and most effective forms of energy protection is to use a bubble of light. This can be of any colour but I usually use gold or white.

Technique 1

This exercise is incredibly simple and only takes a few seconds. You can do it and use it anywhere.

1. Imagine your aura expanding and spreading upwards and outwards. With each breath your aura grows the same way your chakras do.
2. Now imagine a beautiful light surrounding you. It can be any colour you like.

That is it – you are now protected. It is as simple as that.

Technique 2

An even quicker way is invite your dragons in to keep your energy high and clear. In many ways I feel this is a vastly superior way of energy protection.

1. Simply ask your dragon to step forward and protect your space and energy.
2. You should become aware of a presence or a weight behind your back.

Your dragons will always have your back but you do also need to help yourself and ask for their presence to join you, work with you, guide you, etc.

Energy Cleansing

I had a big lesson from the dragons a little while ago on protection and keeping my energy clear. I had fallen foul of a psychic attack. It was not particularly malicious, but it was disrupting my work and my connection. I had become complacent (and probably lazy) with regards to clearing my energy, disconnecting after client sessions and using my protection.

I enlisted the help of a friend as it was not something I could do on my own. I had become aware of something disturbing my connection after having my violet flame attunement. As this attunement is such a high frequency and clear vibration to work with, it showed up like a flashing sign that my connection was not as clear or solid as it had been. Around the same time I had booked a series of sound bath sessions. All of this was subconscious in many ways, and while I knew I was off kilter

I could not put my finger on how. Was I just tired? Was my energy simply a bit flat?

As I worked through clearing my energy, taking a bit of time for me, the rest of my energy system cleared. All I was left with was this vague feeling that something was still off. I was also suffering from awful neck ache so I booked a massage and saw my chiropractor.

I basically went through everything and slowly came to the conclusion that I had an attachment. Yes, I can be a bit dense at times and the dragons do roll their eyes in exasperation with me. Until this point, attachments were not something I had paid a great deal of attention to or thought about. I was aware that others talked of attachments but it had not happened to me personally.

So I asked my friend Amanda (who is a brilliant energy worker) if she could check my energy. Amanda found and removed an attachment from my energy system that was pretty ingrained and had been deliberately sent to block me. It affected my third eye, crown and solar plexus and had been sent to disconnect and disempower me.

Amanda gave me some work to do over the following couple of weeks to ensure my energy was kept clear. I visualized that the gap where the attachment had been removed was refilled with clear bright energy.

There are a number of exercises you can use to keep your energy finely tuned, bright and clear. Any of the exercises below can be adapted to fit in with your regular meditation practice, whether this is weekly or daily. None of these exercises need to be done specifically. They are also really useful if you have had a particularly grotty day and need to shift negative energy – whether this is yours or something you picked up from someone or somewhere else. You can also use it to cleanse rooms, whole buildings or just your energy field and your chakras. Practise it, adapt and use it in any way that suits your needs at the time. Trust your intuition and guidance from your dragons.

Cleansing Visualization

1. Visualize yourself in the space you wish to cleanse.
2. In your mind's eye, see a beautiful sheer blue silk cloth covering the entire area.
3. Visualize the cloth gently lifting off the floor. The cloth is able to pass through every object in the room including you. It will gather up all negative energy that is held in your environment. It will cleanse thoroughly and deeply.
4. As you move upwards taking the cloth up through the building and out through the roof on toward the sky, tie the cloth's four corners together. This will prevent the dross, stress, blockages and negativity from escaping and repolluting you and your atmosphere.
5. Your dragon is waiting for you in the Universe. Invite them to join you and hold the cloth out to them. They will blast a spiral of bright cleansing fiery energy over the cloth, neutralising everything that was held inside it.
6. As your dragon does this, you will see bright sparks of clear crystalline light fall from the ashes of the cloth that gently float down and around you and into the space you have cleared, filling it with vibrant bright energising light.

Another version of this is to clear your own energy body. It is useful to use this to clear your chakras and aura simultaneously.

1. See yourself sitting or standing on a beautiful sheer silk cloth.
2. Sense the silk move through your aura, starting at your feet and moving upwards, slowly cleansing and clearing.
3. Feel the silk start to move up through the soles of your feet, unblocking and cleansing the chakras there.

4. Feel the silk starting to move gently and slowly up through your body and auric field, moving up through your ankles, shins, knees and thighs to your root centre. As the silk moves, it cleanses and clears any negative energy and blockages within you.
5. Gradually take the silk through each part of your body and aura and each chakra in turn.
6. Once you have passed through your crown chakra, tie the silk cloth's four corners together and invite your dragon to join you to cleanse the silk of all negativity held inside it.
7. Observe the transformation take place. As before, notice bright sparks of pure and clear crystalline light fall from the ashes of the cloth that gently float down and around you and into your energy field, filling it with vibrant bright energising light.
8. Once you feel this is complete, carry out a body scan to see how you feel. If you feel different, how do you feel different?

That can be an incredibly powerful meditation and bring many different emotions to the surface. Do not ignore them. Acknowledge and work with them (I cover this in more detail later in the book) and write down everything and anything you feel. If you notice a particular emotion or feeling surfacing you can meditate on it to help heal and clear it.

Of course, you always have a dragon by your side. So ask for their guidance as they are the wisest of the wise. As is the dragons' way, they will show you either directly through meditation or send messages to you through the Universe. This can be via a song on the radio, putting you in the path of a relevant healer or therapist, or discovering that a person within your circle has experienced a similar emotion or problem.

Just remember that you are NOT on your own. It is all about discovering who you are and what you are here to do.

Finally, the very last cleansing meditation is the simplest of all. The dragons are big fans of simplicity.

1. Close your eyes and invite your dragon to join you.
2. Visualize your dragon in front of you and they will begin to form.
3. When you are ready, ask your dragon to clear your energy thoroughly and completely. You can ask them to clear your energy field, your chakras or space or to do it all in one go. As you do so you will see bright fiery dragon breath clearing through your energy system.

Throughout this chapter, you have discovered how to begin your dragon journey through meditation and how to keep yourself grounded and protected and your energy clear.

Over the coming chapters, I will endeavour to continue to take you on a deepening dragon journey, expanding your connection with them.

DRAGON TIP

➤ *GROUNDING – DEEP GROUNDING IS KEY FOR WORKING WITH DRAGON ENERGY.*

➤ *MAINTAIN A CLEAR BRIGHT ENERGY.*

➤ *KEEP A DETAILED WRITTEN RECORD OF YOUR DRAGON EXPERIENCES AND MEDITATIONS.*

➤ *DO NOT BE DISCOURAGED IF YOU DO NOT SEE OR HEAR YOUR DRAGONS.*

CHAPTER

2

Dragon Guides, Teachers and Guardians

As I discussed at the beginning of the book, many of you will have found dragons suddenly arriving in your consciousness. This means they have chosen to work with you. You do not need to make offerings, sacrifices or anything else to honour these beings! Working with dragon is a collaboration, teamwork and a friendship like any other relationship you have in the physical three-dimensional world. It takes effort to maintain friendships and so it is in the spirit world.

The dragons approve and encourage collaboration, particularly for the greater good of the planet and communities. Their roles are varied, and how they work with you will very much depend on your own personal circumstances and interests.

Like spirit guides, your dragons will grow and evolve with you. Some will be with you for a good few years while others will come for a season or two. The only dragon that never changes is your Guardian Dragon so I will start with this one first.

Guardian Dragons

It is worth putting in the time to get to know your Guardian Dragon. Guardian Dragons have a dual role. They are first and foremost your oldest and best friends ever! Secondly they are incredible gatekeepers. They protect you physically and energetically. They will have been with you through every incarnation you have ever experienced on this planet, across other worlds, galaxies and dimensions. In short, they have been with you from _your_ very beginning.

Your Guardian Dragon knows you better than anyone else and quite possibly better than you know yourself. They know all your strengths and weaknesses, what your karmic lessons are and what your soul contract entails. Make friends with them – this will be the best friendship you ever have.

I have seen and heard in recent years that people feel a need to carry out very specific rituals and to be "a worthy person" to invoke a dragon. This, I feel, is really not necessary and implies the person is not good enough to work with or call upon dragons.

First and foremost, the dragons have come back to us now to support and guide us. We do not need to bow and scrape to them or be sycophantic in any way. Be respectful, yes, as you would be with anyone, whether in this, the physical realm, or the spirit world. Treat people, your dragons and spirit guides as you wish to be treated yourself.

If you do specific work such as spirit rescue, energy clearance of homes or land, you can call on your Guardian Dragon to protect you and your space. In fact you can call upon them any time you feel you would like some protection, such as when walking home late at night or travelling on your own.

This is a simple request to invoke your Guardian Dragon: "Guardian Dragon, please step forward to protect me and the space around me, keeping me safe and my energy clear."

You can also call on your Guardian Dragon if you feel you would like a confidence boost in any situation such as an interview or public speaking. They will stand by your side and be rooting for you. Again it is a simple request; ask them to step forward to support you in whichever way you need. This can be either voiced out loud or as a silent thought.

Always keep it simple with the dragons; they do not need lots of explanation. Even if you can't verbalize what you would like, just feel it and send those thoughts and feelings out. The beauty of working with the dragons is you can call upon them at any time to help, guide and support you, and where appropriate to help those you love. The results can be swift and astonishing.

When you ask your dragon to join you this takes place instantaneously even if you are not physically aware of it. You may get a sense of a dragon behind you or feel their wings wrap around you or even see or hear them. You will notice a shift of energy, almost like the air behind and around you has moved or become heavier. There will be a weight at your back and a sense of feeling safe.

Communicating with Dragons

Something to touch on here is that I receive many messages from people who fear they have "lost" their dragon connection. They ask what has happened, what have they done wrong, why have their dragons stopped communicating or joining them in mediation, and so on.

Our dragons do not desert us, but they will step back.

Dragons do understand that life gets in the way and we get sidetracked. They do find it a bit odd that (in their eyes) we have the attention span of a gnat, but they are also (now much more so) tolerant of our obscure ways. When we are ready to focus upon our spiritual path once more, they are there waiting for us to pick up where we left off. They do not judge us or intimidate us, although if they feel we are being particularly stupid we will be in line for a dragon slap.

Another question that crops up time and again is: Can I ask my dragon to help a friend or family member?

This is a bit of grey area as we have no right to interfere in the affairs of others. We do not know what their life path entails or what their personal soul contract is about. And we can't presume to know what is best for them. We may _think_ we know better, but do we?

So in this respect if you know someone is having a truly hard time, ask them if they would like some dragon support and guidance? If they say "yes, please", ask your dragons or theirs to support and guide them as is right for them. But if they say "no", that is the end of it, regardless of what you think or feel. Do not call on the dragons to interfere with another person's life without that person's specific permission to do so. It is rude and none of your business or your place to do so. And you could find yourself on the other end of a dragon slap.

But there is also another way. You can ask their dragons or yours to help someone to help themselves.

I tried this out with someone close to me who had a drug addiction; they would not admit they had a problem or acknowledge their life was spiralling way out of control. They had drug debts, could not hold down a job and were drinking way too much. They were on a rollercoaster to oblivion.

I asked my dragons and their spiritual helpers (they are not aware of their dragons) to help this person to help themselves. To help them find the strength they needed for themselves. I also understood that this may mean their life could go downhill further first.

To say the results were astonishing is an understatement. Within three days they admitted they had a problem, needed help, sought help and got themselves clean. I was astounded by the speed of it all and how well they coped coming out the other side of it all too. Dragons really are quite incredible.

If the person is not ready to help themselves your request will go unheeded. This is not a reflection of you nor your dragons. It is just that person's own life choices, lessons and path in this lifetime. If they are in a place where they are open, willing and ready to seek help, make changes, heal and grow, they will be able to do so. If they are not, nothing will change for them. And you can't interfere energetically with the dragons.

Remember that what you may feel is best for someone is not necessarily so; you could well be interfering with their life path, life lessons or karmic debt. And doing it for someone's highest good, talking to the other person's higher self, does not cut it with the dragons. You have been warned!

Meet your Guardian Dragon

You may like to record the following meditation and play it back or work with a couple of friends. One of you can read it aloud while the others meditate and then swap. Once you are all familiar with it, you will be able to do this or any of the meditations within the book without guidance.

To begin this exercise, start with using either the extended chakra or heart-centred meditation from chapter one to ensure that you are grounded and present. Once this is complete, continue to the following meditation.

1. You find yourself in a forest glade. The trees stand tall around you, watching like sentinels. What are they like? What type are they? Can you identify them? Do they have their leaves or are they evergreens? Get a feel of the time of day and time of year, absorbing everything and connecting with all your senses. Feel the air and smell the freshness of your environment. What is the ground like beneath your feet? Is it stony, grassy, wet or dry, hard or soft, for example? Take a

few minutes to really notice it, feel it and connect with it. Can you see it, smell it and hear it – or do you simply know it?

2. As you look around, you notice a lake and waterfall on one side of the glade. You feel yourself being drawn toward the lake almost as if an invisible cord is pulling you gently forward, and you feel you need to take off your shoes as you reach the sandy shore. In front of you, nine stepping stones traverse the lake toward the waterfall. For the first time you notice the gushing noise of the falling water.

3. As you take your first steps on the stepping stones, allow all your worldly thoughts to drop away. Once you reach the other side, stand under the waterfall and let it wash over you, allowing it to cleanse your aura, chakras, body and mind so your final thoughts can be washed away.

4. When you are ready leave the curtain of falling water and step into the cave behind it. Slowly your eyes become accustomed to the dim light and you become aware of drawings on the walls. Take a few moments to look at them. The walls appear wet, yet when touched, your hand comes away dry.

5. You have a sense that you are being watched yet you feel safe. You _are_ safe. You sense a movement and turn around in time to see a tail disappearing along a passageway you had not noticed until now. As you follow the tail, the sloping ground takes you steadily downwards, gently going deeper and deeper into the cave. Burning torches in the cave walls light your way forward.

6. Eventually the passageway opens out and you find yourself in a great cavern and standing on another sandy shore. There is a lake, a small boat and light shining in from above, a short distance away, reflecting in the water. The presence you followed shows their self to you. Welcome to your Guardian Dragon.

7. Your dragon steps forward and you regard each other, looking deeply into each other's eyes for a while. You can feel a deep recognition stirring deeply within you, like coming home. Slowly the dragon drops their head to yours and you connect forehead to forehead, third eye to third eye. This is the dragon's way and their formal greeting.

8. Once your dragon lifts their head you have the opportunity to see them fully. What do they look like? How big are they? What is their colouring? What colour are their eyes? How do they feel? What do you sense about them? Spend as much time here with them as feels right. Look and feel for as much detail as you can.

9. They invite you to go with them. Journey with them and explore, ask your Guardian questions about your life, previous lives or anything else you would like to know until you feel your time with them is complete. When you are finished, remember to thank them.

When you are ready to come back to this world, wiggle your fingers and toes, have a gentle stretch and softly open your eyes, allowing your vision and focus to return gently. Quietly do a mental check in with yourself to see how you feel.

When you are fully back from your meditation, write down as much information as you can remember about what you saw and felt, any smells or sounds and information from your dragon encounters. Be as clear and as specific as you can be in your recollection. As you write, a deeper understanding and clarity will come to you. Make sure you have a glass of water to hand as you write up your experiences in your journal.

Remember to close down once you are completely finished.

Soul Contracts and Life Purpose

Your Guardian Dragon knows exactly why you are here (your life purpose) and what opportunities you will encounter. They also know how you are likely to react – after all, they know you better than anyone, including you. Your Guardian will guide all the way if asked to do so but like all spiritual beings will not interfere with your free will.

Akashic Records

The Akashic records are also known as the Halls of Learning or the Great Library. This is a huge library where every soul's lifetimes are contained in enormous tomes. Your book holds all the information about every incarnation you have ever had (and those still to come). It also contains information about your current life; both you and your Guardian have access to this information. Although in truth your Guardian already knows this information, it could be helpful for you to view it. This information can reveal your soul contract, what you agreed to before you incarnated and what you wished to experience for you personally or to support another soul who is a part of your soul group or family. These are sometimes tough lessons or agreements to accept and follow through.

You may have noticed here that we are not being all light and fluffy. Life is at times a challenge and the dragons are here to support us all through the good times and the hard ones.

The dragons also talk of the shadow self or shadow work – this work can be hard but we do not learn or grow spiritually by being all love and light and bypassing our more difficult thoughts, feelings, emotions or experiences. This is why we have dragons at our side. They support and guide us and at times carry us if needed.

Akashic Record Meditation

Before you begin the following meditation take yourself through the heart-centred meditation in chapter one. Once you are ready, begin the following meditation to travel to the Halls of Learning with your Guardian Dragon.

1. You find yourself on a deserted beach just as the sun is rising on the horizon. You can hear the gentle lapping of the waves on the shore. You watch the waves for a time as they roll in and out. It is quite mesmerising.

2. You lift your eyes to the emerging sun on the horizon. From the waves far out to sea, a shape begins to form. You recognize this as your own Guardian Dragon as it makes its way across the sky toward you.

3. The dragon lands surprisingly gently and quietly in front of you. You study each other for a few moments. The dragon drops their head to yours, connecting forehead to forehead, third eye to third eye, as is the dragon's way.

4. Your dragon asks you if you are ready and invites you to climb aboard. You settle yourself slightly in front of their great wings, feeling surprisingly secure. Within a blink of an eye you are airborne.

5. Your dragon takes you higher, higher and higher. Eventually he begins to slow and descend and you find yourself in the grounds of the most beautiful gardens you have ever seen. The scent of the flowers, the vibrancy of colour, the way the light and shade dances. You are immersed in a vibrancy of colour and the sights, sounds and scents that fill your senses.

6. Your Guardian beckons you to follow him through the gardens toward a striking-looking building. You follow

them and find yourself in a vast library, filled floor to ceiling with books. An ornate table and chair sits in the middle of the room with the largest book you have ever seen. This is your book, the book of your lifetimes. You leaf through the brittle, older pages, taking in snippets of information of previous lives and past contracts until you reach the pages you are looking for.

7. Spend as much time as you need to read about your life and experiences. Remember your Guardian is with you to help you with anything you do not understand, so ask them to clarify for you.

8. When you are ready, leave the library and climb aboard your dragon so they can carry you home.

9. Remember to close down once you are finished.

You have now met your Guardian Dragon, so it is time to introduce you to some of the other dragons.

Dragon Guides

A few years ago we were house hunting. We wanted a project: an old house in need of renovation and with a little bit of land with it. The dragons had been quiet for a while as I was completely engrossed in the physical world and I was working within the building industry.

In May 2013 we found the perfect spot and house. It needed work but had a large garden with enough parking for our needs. As we stood in the overgrown garden of this run down cottage the dragons joined me that morning, telling me, "This is your house, and we will pick up where we left off. Now is the time to bring us into the world."

What I now understand is that the dragons guided me into the jobs I needed with the right people to learn from and the connections and companies I would need later on. And, of course, without working in the building industry none of what I do now with the dragons would have been possible. They guided me and paved the way for what would transpire years later!

There is no way we could have undertaken such a large project if I had not understood what it entailed – from bat surveys to planning permission to completion of a major building project.

The dragons leave me awestruck and speechless! They really are quite incredible beings!

Our dragon guides are very much like close friends. The ones who will tell you the truth and be honest and reliable. The type of friend you call up in the middle of the night and know they will be there for you as you would be for them. I often think of them as incredibly forthright and on occasions strict but fair parents. I guess really the dragons show us how to be a good parent to ourselves!

A dragon guide will support you as you traverse the ups and downs of your physical life and guide you through if you ask for their help as discussed earlier in the chapter. Dragon guides have a spiritual element to them, of course, and there are also those that are a dragon teacher and guide rolled into one.

A dragon guide will encourage you to grow and push through your comfort zone and believe in yourself, to leave your self-imposed doubts behind, to feel the fear and do it anyway, to face your crippling phobias, take that promotion, try out a new hairdo, go on that retreat you yearn to. In short, they will help, guide and support you with any aspect of your physical life on Earth.

All they ask is that you take the steps you need to make it happen, as they can't do it all for you. Look out for all the coincidences and synchronicities and for signs and messages from the world around you. They will talk to you and guide you. Your job is to listen, watch and act upon it. They ask you to be brave, courageous and begin to trust yourself.

Meet Your Dragon Guide

Retreat to your sacred working and meditation space and follow the steps below, carrying out the heart-centred meditation from chapter one first. You can use the following meditation for both your dragon guide and dragon teacher.

1. It is early evening and you are out walking in a wide open space. The sun is setting and you marvel as the sky progresses through the colours of orange, red and purple hues as you watch it set on the horizon.
2. The sky begins to darken and you watch the first stars of the evening begin to twinkle into light. As you watch, one of them burns more brightly and appears to be moving across the sky and coming toward you.
3. The little star becomes a pulsing bright white ball of light, getting large and larger the closer it gets. It lands a few feet away, glimmering, shimmering and throwing out a pale whitish blue light. You feel yourself being drawn toward it and you tentatively put your hand out to touch it. As you do so the light falls away. From it emerges the most magnificent dragon you have ever encountered.
4. You spend a moment regarding each other. The dragon drops their head to yours, connecting third eye to third eye.
5. Your dragon lifts their head and looks deeply into your eyes. You recognize each other on a deeper level. You see the Universe, world and all that exists reflected back at you. You are able to sense their power, majesty and honourability in those eyes. They are deep souls who care deeply for mankind.

6. Your dragon tells you that they have something they wish to share with you. You climb on their back, feeling strangely safe perched just in front of their wings. With a great flap of those giant wings you are airborne. Your journey with your dragon is yours and yours alone. Take your time and enjoy the experience.

When you are ready to come back to this world, wiggle your fingers and toes, have a gentle stretch and softly open your eyes, allowing your vision and focus to return gently. Remember to thank your dragons for their care and time and for guiding and sharing with you.

When you are fully back from your meditation, write down as much information as you can remember about what you saw and felt, any smells or sounds and information from your dragon encounters. Be as clear and specific as you can be in your recollection. As you write, a deeper understanding and clarity will come to you. Make sure you have a glass of water to hand as you write up your experiences in your journal. When you are finished, remember to close down energetically.

Dragon as Spiritual Teachers

Dragons are among the best spiritual teachers I have ever worked with. They have guided me to, taught me or given me as a download almost everything held within the pages of this book.

Below is what one of my dragon guides, Joshua the Speaker, told me about why we have dragons and why they are back with us at this time.

DRAGON TALK

"*We came in droves to support our counterparts, the archangels, in the destruction of what you call 9/11. Our angels wept at the pain you inflict upon each other, and they needed our support with carrying the dying, the wounded and those who had passed in such terror.*

"*Gradually people of Earth are waking up to our presence. There are those enlightened ones who have always been aware of our presence and there are those who are only waking up to it now. We welcome you all as you are about to begin a new phase in your spiritual awakening on Earth.*

"*We, the dragons, link to every culture and civilisation throughout history – we date back to time immemorial. Yes, some of us have links to Atlantis but not all of us. We have been around this planet since the dawn of time.*"

As a footnote to Joshua's words he ended with the following:

"*Dragons aren't keen on cheesecake.*"

I will talk more about the Dragon of Atlantis further on in the book.

DRAGON TIP

⫸ *YOUR DRAGON TEACHER AND DRAGON GUIDE CAN BE THE SAME DRAGON.*

⫸ *REMEMBER THAT DRAGONS CAN AND DO STEP BACK FROM US FROM TIME TO TIME, ESPECIALLY IF WE NEED TO DEAL WITH OUR PHYSICAL THREE-DIMENSIONAL WORLD.*

⫸ *YOU CAN ASK YOUR DRAGONS FOR GUIDANCE AND SUPPORT.*

CHAPTER

3

Dragon as Healers

All the dragons carry an element of healing, but some more so than others. Some of them carry a shamanic energy, in particular Asclepius and the Avebury Matriarch (from my Dragon Path Oracle deck). This is the vibration they first come to me on and therefore they carry the underworld type of energy.

Over the years the dragons have taught me that much of our spiritual evolution comes from our own personal healing journey. When we embark upon this journey we discover a deeper sense of self and self-awareness, compassion, empathy, non-judgement and more. Everyone has their own personal strengths they work toward and "internal clutter" to work on.

Self-Awareness

As our awareness of "self" expands, we learn to recognize our triggers, shortcomings and flaws. From here we begin our healing, working with our shadow side. As we heal we grow, and this in turn ripples out into the collective consciousness and supports humanity as a whole. From this healing standpoint, over time we are able to glimpse the bigger picture; this will be unique for each of us.

Take for example a lack of self-confidence. This is most likely hidden in an old wound. It could be from a significant or insignificant event or events. The "how and why" is not necessarily important for everyone but the healing that takes place around it is. A lack of self-confidence is likely to have numerous layers to it. And so the work begins ...

Here you may like to ask the dragon Confidence from my deck to help guide you to heal or to discover ways to help you begin to believe in yourself and trust yourself. This is because all of these things are connected with and tied to a lack of self-confidence. Or you may like to ask your dragon guide to support and guide you as you work through these things yourself.

The guidance can take any form – from being led toward a particular practitioner/healer, such as a counsellor or someone who uses Bach Flower Remedies. You may be guided toward reiki or other energy healers. All of it will be relevant and useful to your journey.

Remember the dragons always have your back no matter what. Your job under their tutelage is to listen and gain greater awareness of yourself and the Universe at large.

The simplest way to gain self-awareness is through mindfulness, which opens up a whole new world. We learn through mindfulness that there is only "now" – this moment. The dragons led me along this pathway a few years ago.

Our world is not outside of us. It *is* us – a reflection of us. Ever the mirror!

The Underworld

The underworld tends to show us what we need to work on and can reveal our subconscious. We may have fears, phobias, addictions, anxiety and more. Working in the underworld is not to be undertaken lightly and is best embarked upon with an experienced teacher and ideally a shaman/woman.

In my deck, *The Dragon Path Oracle*, three dragons are healers. Two of them carry the shamanic energy discussed above and the third is energy- and vibration-based.

The meditations in this chapter are safe for you to try at home. But for anything deeper, especially from an underworld and shamanic perspective, I sincerely ask you to seek help from a qualified and trained shaman, especially if you are a novice.

The dragons ask us to be the very best human beings we can be. They ask us to find tolerance, drop judgements and embrace compassion and understanding. They are not particularly fond of love 'n' light – it tends to rattle them. They are beings of great integrity and authenticity, and love 'n' light frequently bypasses those more uncomfortable feelings we like to sidestep. That, my dear reader, is not healing; it is ducking and diving your deeper inner feelings and at times emotions. And it most definitely does not support your spiritual evolution or growth.

When it comes to healing with any of the dragons, there are a number of approaches you can use. These are discussed in detail over the coming pages.

Healing with Asclepius

Asclepius is an incredibly diverse healing dragon. His specialism is working with those who heal in and with the natural world. In short, he works with therapists who use plants for healing such as herbalists, aromatherapists, flower remedy practitioners, as well as vets.

He is the son of Apollo and known as the god of medicine (although he is not as well known as Hippocrates). Asclepius was brought up by Chiron the wounded healer. Interesting stuff! It makes sense that he also works with those of us who work as healers as we traverse and work through the shadow self.

DRAGON TALK

Asclepius's opening words to me when we met many years ago were:

"Your caduceus is wrong. The staff has one snake. This is for transformation and power. This is the true meaning of healing."

There are many ways to embrace and work with the shadow self and numerous pointers that your shadow side is rearing its head for acknowledgement and healing. But how do you know when your shadow is showing itself?

A big giveaway is when something triggers you or pushes your buttons. Queues in the supermarket, rude drivers, someone perceived as inconsiderate, people in power, the them and us attitude, the haves and the have nots. Jealousy, anger, judgement, frustration, guilt, fear and racism – all of these are an indication of pain that we carry around within us. And yes, all these things can make us uncomfortable and reactive.

Each and every one of us has a lifetime of experiences, judgements and ideals that we hold on to. And it is these that are frequently a clue to the healing work that needs to be done when working with the shadow self.

Note: There are no finite or definitive rules when it comes to healing and understanding our shadow side.

Seeking Healing Help from Asclepius

An obvious approach to healing involves working with Asclepius in meditation. But before we go there, there are a couple of other exercises you may like to try first.

If you know what you need, for example a brilliant massage therapist, homeopath, counsellor or herbalist, but you do not know anyone, you can simply ask Asclepius for his guidance, either speaking out loud or phrasing your questions silently.

You may find it helpful when you first begin asking the dragons for help to write down your requests. By writing it down you begin to truly feel what you need support, healing, guidance or help with. It may go something like this: "Asclepius guide me to the perfect therapist to help with [list here what you need help with. This may be aches and pains, migraines, allergies, hormonal or emotional issues, etc.]"

Do not be surprised once you begin to delve into writing your question about what you thought you require morphs into something else entirely. By *voicing* what you require, you are connecting with your body and paying it full attention. It may take a few attempts to get your question written down in such a way that feels right and actually describes how you feel, your pain and your thoughts and emotions around it. Follow what feels right. Your question does not have to be perfect. The dragons do already know what you need but will not interfere with your life path without being invited to help.

If nothing else, the above exercise is a great way for you to get to know yourself better. It helps to untangle your thoughts and feelings around a particular topic, giving you some clarity. Try to keep it simple though. Asclepius will take you by the hand and lead you where you need to go but you must play your part.

If you do not have a clear dragon connection such as clairaudience, the dragons will use the Universe and the world around you to communicate with you. So be on the lookout for synchronicities; those odd coincidences that crop up exactly when you need them, pointing you in the right direction.

The meditation described below is designed to take you on a healing journey with Asclepius. If you are experiencing any form of ill health, feeling poorly or are just generally out of sorts, this meditation will support you.

Healing Meditation with Asclepius

Begin with using the heart-centred meditation in chapter one, ensuring that you are grounded and present.

1. You find yourself in the cave dwelling of Asclepius. The light is dim and the walls are bumpy yet smooth to touch. They feel cool under your fingers, yet the cave itself is warm. You notice veins of crystals running along the walls. There is a fresh scent of pine and lavender that clears your senses.

2. Asclepius invites you to draw closer to him. He has laid out a circle of stones large enough for you to lie down in. The floor is soft and sandy and there are soft rugs waiting for you. Once you are settled you have his full attention and can feel his gaze upon you.

3. He asks what ails you. As you tell him, he listens and watches you closely, taking in every nuance of your speech, facial expressions and body language. You feel like you are being properly heard and a great weight shifts within you.

4. As you drift with the sounds and smells of the cave, Asclepius sets to work on you. You notice points of warmth or coolness around your body. He wafts scents around specific areas of your being and images of certain plants float through your mind. He draws colour into your aura and lays crystals around

you. He works quietly and steadily, murmuring and reassuring you.

5. Stay here with Asclepius for as long as you feel you need to.

When you are ready to come back to this world, wiggle your fingers and toes, have a gentle stretch and softly open your eyes, allowing your vision and focus to return gently. Quietly do a mental check in with yourself to see how you feel.

When you are fully back from your meditation write down as much information as you can remember on what you saw, felt, any smells or sounds and information from your dragon encounters. Be as clear and as specific as you can be in your recollection. As you write, a deeper understanding and clarity will come to you. Make sure you have a glass of water to hand as you write up your experiences in your journal.

The Avebury Matriarch

Often within families there are disruptive or negatively repeating patterns passed down the family line frequently from mother to daughter. If left unchecked these patterns can disrupt the course of a life or even lifetimes. They become stuck within our DNA and are passed from generation to generation, who are destined to play them out and powerless to change them. Here the dragon Avebury Matriarch invites us to explore where these patterns began.

The tightly held wounds within your energy system were carried forward from your ancestors. These could be anything from arguments that have wounded deeply and resounded through the ages to curses, guilt, anger, revenge, abandonment and so on. There are no hard and fast rules. You may have a particular reoccurring family pattern or issue that you wish to release and work through with your ancestors. This is your space; you know what you are ready for and what needs healing.

The Avebury Matriarch will guide you to meet the ancestors who will be most beneficial to your life path. These ancestors may be recent or ancient and you may journey to more than one group of them. They will all have a valuable and positive impact on what you are ready to hear, understand and release. You will journey with the Matriarch back through the depths of time to explore anything that is stuck, blocking you from healing yourself or your family on a deeper level. Many of the dragons are of a shamanic nature, hence the use of the word journey rather than meditation.

Go wherever you feel guided. You may feel you need to offer forgiveness and absolve or be absolved of certain responsibilities. This is limitless. Follow what feels right for you and be guided by the Avebury Matriarch.

Ancestral Healing Meditation with the Avebury Matriarch

Begin with using the heart-centred meditation from chapter one, ensuring that you are grounded and present.

1. Imagine yourself within an ancient stone circle that has energy and magic that makes your skin gently tingle. It is early evening and the stars are beginning to blink into life in the velvety night sky. The crescent moon is slowly making her way skyward from low on the horizon.
2. You kick off your shoes and connect with the ancient lands you find yourself in. You scrunch the grass under

your toes, enjoying how cool it feels. You brush your fingers across the stones as you pass by them and notice how the texture and coarseness of each stone is different. You become aware of a gentle humming; the stones are talking to you and each other, welcoming you to their inner circle. Each stone has a story to tell, each one being a gateway into your ancestral past.

3. You feel yourself being drawn toward a particular megalith. The stone begins to shimmer and becomes almost transparent. You put your hand out to touch it but your hand passes straight through. You pull your hand out and everything returns to how it was before.

4. You feel the gentle tug of the stone and step forward into it. Before you is a gentle downward slope. You are in a cave-like structure with high ceilings and flame torches attached to walls lighting your way. You go deeper and deeper along the cave's path, eventually reaching a large underground antechamber. Around the edge of the antechamber are a number of doors, each one with a coloured glow as though it is lit from the other side.

5. You are drawn to one particular door. As you approach, the door swings silently open and you walk through to find a group of your ancestors sitting around a large fire, mumming gently among themselves. You spend a few minutes becoming accustomed to the light and taking in the scene: the smell of the wood smoke, the earth or cooking, maybe, listening to the fire crackle and spark and the murmuring of voices.

6. The ancestors look up and greet you, beckoning you forward and making a space for you to sit within their circle. You spend a few minutes surveying each member of the group and may recognize some of them at a soul level. Avebury Matriarch is on the periphery of the group, observing. She is there to step in if you require her support, to transmute anything that may need a little extra power.

7. Spend as much time as you need with your family, talking, sharing and healing the past. Note any feelings and the era they are from. Ask what has brought you all together. These souls now have wisdom that they may not have possessed during their incarnations on Earth. They too wish to release the burdens and constraints that have been rippling through the family. Forgiveness may be sought and given, a depth of understanding may arise, compassion for those who carried the pain. Each of you is as unique as your family.

8. When you are ready to leave, the Avebury Matriarch steps forward and draws herself up to her full height. She asks each of you if you are ready to leave behind the pain, anguish, guilt, sorrow and more? Are you all ready to be released from the tendrils of pain that have wound their way through generation to generation?

9. Slowly and gently she blows a healing breath that weaves its way around all of you, encasing you in a pale coloured mist. You feel its purifying, cleansing and releasing energy. You sense old wounds start to heal as each person is released from the bonds that held them fast. The air pressure feels lighter. Your ancestors have a glow around them and then slowly they begin to fade.

10. As you turn to leave, Avebury Matriarch has a final word for you before leading you back to the stone circle. Once more you find yourself in the antechamber, and the sconces on the wall are beginning to burn down. You make your way back along the passageway and up the slope leading back to the stones above.

11. Once back in the open air you take one deep healing and clearing breath. You feel like a weight has been lifted and slowly your physical senses are returning. You can feel your feet on the floor and your hands on your lap.

When you are ready to come back to this world, wiggle your fingers and toes, have a gentle stretch and softly open your eyes, allowing your vision and focus to return gently. Quietly do a mental check in with yourself to see how you feel.

When you are fully back from your meditation write down as much information as you can remember about what you saw and felt, any smells or sounds and information from your dragon encounters. Be as clear and as specific as you can be in your recollection. As you write, a deeper understanding and clarity will come to you. Make sure you have a glass of water to hand as you write up your experiences in your journal.

This particular meditation may take a few days to process so take your time to think about how you feel and be gentle with yourself for a few days. Keeping a journal is incredibly useful here; I cover more about this in the next chapter.

If you have particularly strong patterns you wish to work through, it may take more than one meditation with the Avebury Matriarch to break through all the layers and barriers, so be patient with yourself. Be aware that you may need the support of a qualified practitioner to help you over a specific hurdle if you feel you are stuck.

About the Healer

The Healer works in particular with energy workers, so those who practise any kind of energy healing such as reiki, crystal healing, sound healing etc. He acts as a guide and at times a teacher within their work, helping them with clients.

Just as with Asclepius, the Healer's role is dual aspect; he supports those actively working and learning their skills in the energy realm and also supports those seeking help from those who work with energy. You can also call upon the Healer for healing for yourself. The following meditation guides you in receiving a healing from him. You can use this meditation as often as you feel you need to.

Meditation with the Healer

Begin with using the heart-centred meditation from chapter one, ensuring that you are grounded and present.

1. Visualize yourself floating. You may be on an enormous soft downy bed or high in the sky on a light fluffy cloud or even on a body of lapping warm water moving gently with the motion.
2. As you lie there enjoying the feeling of weightlessness, embrace your sensation of freedom. Allow the lightness to permeate every cell of your being as you sink deeper and deeper into calm bliss.
3. You are joined by the Healer. He takes great care in looking at you, noting where you feel out of sorts and off kilter.
4. Once he has finished his inspection he steps back and begins to blow gentle fiery breath on you, paying particular attention to the areas where you feel a little off.
5. Notice the colour of his breath and any sensations you experience.
6. Stay here for as long as you feel you need to.

When you are ready to come back to this world, wiggle your fingers and toes, have a gentle stretch and softly open your eyes, allowing your vision and focus to return gently. Quietly do a mental check in with yourself to see how you feel.

When you are fully back from your meditation write down as much information as you can remember about what you saw and felt, any smells or sounds and information from your dragon encounters. Be as clear and as specific as you can be in your recollection. As you write, a deeper understanding and clarity will come to you. Make sure you have a glass of water to hand as you write up your experiences in your journal.

It is useful to look at the colour of the dragon's breath.

» Green is generally considered to be the overall healing colour.

» Blue is to do with clear communication; I feel it is a balancing colour.

» Red in a healing sense is used for an energy boost.

» Yellow helps to shift the blues.

» Orange encourages creativity.

» Purple is the colour of spirit.

There are many other colours, of course, so keep a note of them and how you felt and what you experienced during each meditation. Over time you will begin to build your own repertoire of what the colours mean to you.

We will look at dragon and colour in more detail in chapter five.

DRAGON TIP

» *CALL UPON DRAGONS FOR HEALING.*

» *WITH UNDERSTANDING COMES HEALING.*

» *HEALING CAN TAKE MANY FORMS.*

CHAPTER

4

Dragons and the Chakras

When discussing the concept of the book with my editor, she asked me if the dragons connect to individual chakras. This was a bit of curveball to me and not one I had previously considered. So I duly sat with the dragons, thinking to myself, "No, they probably don't," but you know what? They do! And once more the dragons show how they are adept teachers in getting their message across in any way they can.

Quite some time ago when I was preparing to write this book, the dragons asked me to spend time revisiting and sitting with the chakras to explore these more deeply and gain a deeper connection and understanding of them. So over a course of about a week I did this.

I have since discovered that there is a dragon for each chakra. Initially I resisted this idea (as is my way). But one day while I was out dog walking with a girlfriend I was talking to her about it and then the entire concept came in with such clarity that I began joining all the dots together. Some of the dragons from the previous chapter connect in here too.

Information Highway

Your chakras are a part of your light body, which I talk about in more detail in chapter 13. These are an important part of your energetic information highway. Messages pass to and from you all day every day via your chakras and your aura although you may not be consciously aware of this happening.

With this in mind it is important that your energetic system, your information highway, is kept as clear and bright as you possibly can. There are a huge variety of thoughts and topics about keeping both of your systems (bodily and energy) clear and as high frequency and vibration as possible.

I feel it is down to personal choice whether you drink caffeinated drinks, smoke, consume alcohol, eat meat, fish, dairy, wheat, sugar, eat raw or junk food. But do not be surprised that as you embark upon this journey with the dragons you find yourself making different lifestyle choices. The key is to listen to your body. At the end of this chapter I will add in a cleansing visualization.

Root Centre

This is your Earth connection and the powerhouse of everything you can achieve. It is the foundation of your life; your truth of who you are and all you can be. Every success or failure sits here waiting to be explored. Failure is frequently perceived as a negative. Whereas in fact it shows you where you can grow, learn and develop greater skills and understandings.

Safety begins in the root centre and your root is what sustains you. Motivation begins here; it is the root of everything you do in life including trusting yourself. It is the chakra of potential and your pure truth.

Incidentally all the other centres are built upon this one. If the root is out of kilter in any way it puts pressure and strain upon the other three chakra centres above it. The dragons said to me that you do not build a house from the roof down, you build from the ground up. Therefore your connection should be to yourself and the Earth first and foremost before thinking about working with or for spirit.

The dragon curled up in the root centre is a bright clear ruby red – she is Earth Dragon. This makes total sense as our root chakra is our connection to Earth. Our existence here on Earth depends upon the Earth, and all life begins in the dark. Think of the seeds we sow and bulbs we plant into the body of Mother Earth herself.

Sacral Centre

The passion and energy of the root centre is passed up to the sacral chakra. While your root chakra is about learning to trust yourself and believe in yourself, the sacral centre is where your creativity sits – the space of expression including self-expression and the beginning of self-belief. If you have built upon your potential from the root with the energy of the sacral, you have the opportunity to express freely and wisely in whichever discipline draws you, such as music, art, poetry, dance, science and even spirituality.

Babies are nurtured here in more ways than one. Here are the baby steps you take with a piece of artwork or a song maybe. The first tentative steps taken as a new healer or reader, the germination of an idea, all begin life in the sacral centre. Self-care and nurturing is held here along with caring for others. For an idea to thrive you need to care of yourself and acknowledge that you need to be cared for.

In the sacral centre you begin to identify with yourself more fully and view how you feel about yourself. You need to be aware of how you treat yourself (back to self-care) and think about yourself but also how you talk to yourself in both negative and positive ways.

Resolve lives in the sacral chakra too. This is the foundation of your willpower. If you think about this it makes perfect sense as willpower can be weakened or strengthened by positive or negative self-talk. This is where you actually begin to truly identify with yourself.

Fire Dragon is found in the sacral chakra. This is the fire of an idea, the forming of plans. Her colour is amber.

Navel Centre

The navel centre is the home of your full-on personal powerhouse, identity and willpower. It contains your ability to change the course of your life, with the energy, power, resolve and momentum to take you forward. Here is where you take on the full responsibility of your life and the route your life takes.

Your internal strength and resilience find their home here. The amount of resilience you have depends on the balance and health of the previous chakras. The root and sacral chakras set you up energetically to take the power of yourself into your own hands. If these are out of whack, your navel centre will not be as powerful as you need it to be to deal with everything that life may throw at you. The navel is also where the healing and forgiveness of self and others begins its journey.

Your full-on dragon power resides here. She is called Power Dragon (for obvious reasons) and her colour is silver.

Solar Plexus Chakra

The solar plexus is where your authenticity sits. If you think about the three previous chakra centres, how each builds and flows into the next, it makes sense that the "real you" begins to make itself known fully to the outside world here.

The power of expression begins in the sacral centre and you begin to draw up that energy into your navel as you learn to take responsibility for your life, actions, abilities and strengths. For the solar plexus to take you into full adulthood, to be who and what you are fully capable of, the previous centres need to be working at an optimum. The inner work of healing and self-mastery needs to be underway (and this is a constant journey of self-discovery).

Self-belief (or lack of it) shows itself clearly here as you step up and out into the world doing what you love. As you are acknowledging your fears and doubts and working through them you begin to fulfil your spirit contract and take the steps into your authentic power even if those around you doubt you. When all these chakras are in full alignment you are also in full alignment and you will begin to notice when you are not.

In many ways the solar plexus is where the magic happens. It is the centre that helps take you forward and bring to light all of your talents, a little like alchemy.

All the chakras mentioned above play a part in your connection to yourself and the Earth. When you are connected to you, you are more likely to be grounded.

Here you find your dragon of authenticity with her vibrant gold colouring.

Heart Chakra

Now we come to the bridge between earthly matters, grounding and being present to the connection with the spiritual realms. Your compassion for yourself and others is found in the heart chakra – and knowing is the key. The fullness of wisdom shows itself here, and understanding to great depths.

Self-forgiveness and deeper self-healing all take place within the heart. The heart chakra is also the filter and balancer of earthly and spiritual matters. The dragons frequently talk of being heart centred or sinking into your heart.

The heart is where you are able to be your full authentic self, knowing who and what you are and where you are going. It is about accepting and loving yourself "warts 'n' all", as the saying goes. It is the full-on confidence and self-assuredness that began to show itself in the solar plexus. This can be expressed in many ways and is unique for each of us. It is also the pivotal point of spirit connection and inner truth.

You will find your dragon of compassion here. She is compassion for everything, including yourself, and her colour is translucent white.

Do you see how each of the chakras link backwards and forwards with one and other? The following three chakras are all linked in the same way as the previous chakras were linked, with the heart being the balancer in the middle.

Throat Chakra

The throat chakra is your point of communication and verbalisation. It houses your ability to speak clearly, voice your truth and acknowledge your emotions, feelings and thoughts. This is where you stand up for yourself verbally rather than bite your tongue, speaking with clarity, integrity and compassion.

The dragons remind us that to speak with integrity and humility we first need to learn to listen with our full attention. So here in the throat chakra, which is traditionally associated with speaking, you also learn the lesson of fully hearing rather than simply half listening. You learn to understand and appreciate what is being heard without glossing over or muffling it out with your own mind chatter. This internal mind chatter can drown out your ability to hear completely.

To hear dragon or communicate with dragons effectively, the internal noise you make needs to be turned down a few decibels. The dragons ask that you become more aware of your self-talk. You know the kind of thing – calling yourself silly, stupid, useless, for example.

We all talk about being kind to others but that kindness (especially self-talk) starts with you first. When you recognize the self-talk you can also start to recognize self-limiting beliefs. So here your awareness of self deepens.

The dragon of the throat is the dragon of awareness. Her colour is aquamarine.

Third Eye Chakra

Our third eye is our clairvoyant eye. It is frequently where we "see" the other worlds and it enables you to "see" to the heart of the matter. This chakra connects and gives weight to the head, heart and gut theory. That knowingness.

Here you learn discernment of this world and the other worlds. Your journey began way back in the root chakra with your foundations. Here the dragons guide you about your ego mind and your fear mind and you become increasingly aware of your inner dialogue and the impact it can have on your spiritual development.

The third eye also links directly with your heart – your centre of truth. Over time you learn to discern what is real, ego, BS and so on, with your deepening connection to your third eye. And once more there is a link to the previous throat chakra. Here you become more deeply aware of your mind chatter and how it drowns out your spiritual connections.

This is also our point of dragon (and spirit) communication. The dragons talk about mindfulness or to use their words "quiet mind". We are not aware most of the time of the conversations we have with ourselves, going over the "what ifs". Your connection to the dragons carries greater clarity as your mind learns to quieten down.

The dragon that resides here is the dragon of clarity. Her colour is lilac.

Crown Chakra

The crown links back directly to the root chakra, so if you are fully heart centred as the dragons ask you to be you will also be grounded and present. Your dragon connection is far clearer and so are your mind and thoughts. Your body and mind will thank you for the clarity and calm that evolve from doing this work.

Here in the crown chakra the balance of the throat chakra and third eye chakra come into their own and form the full clear connection to the other worlds, not just the dragons. The information gained from being heart centred filters up to crown chakra to be translated in any way that you can relate to. The crown chakra acts as the interpreter of everything you experience.

The dragon who resides here is Gnosis. Her colour is platinum.

Incidental notes: If you find yourself being overwhelmed for extended periods of time or you are constantly exhausted, the chakras begin to run low on fuel and in time become depleted. The energy of the root chakra will keep the sacral going and filter up to each of the chakras for as long as it can until eventually they all run out of steam. The root will keep its own energy ticking over but on fumes, so to speak.

Dragon Chakras

As discussed earlier, each chakra has a dragon counterpart. So once more we will be starting at the root chakra and this time connecting to the energy of the dragon that resides there.

You will be invited to access and activate your full dragon power, connecting to each chakra and dragon. You will learn to feel the energy of the dragon who resides there, how they feel and what work you and they are required to do together.

Through meditation you will connect and invite each dragon to activate the new colours and frequency associated with each chakra. As we go through each chakra you will be asking yourself and your dragon specific questions and taking note of any differences in energy.

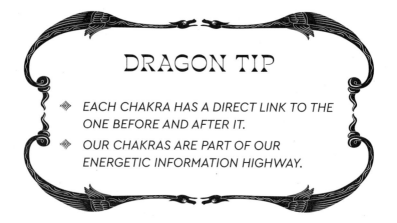

DRAGON TIP

➤ *EACH CHAKRA HAS A DIRECT LINK TO THE ONE BEFORE AND AFTER IT.*

➤ *OUR CHAKRAS ARE PART OF OUR ENERGETIC INFORMATION HIGHWAY.*

Meet Your Chakra Dragons

As in the previous exercises begin with head and heart meditation from chapter one. When you are ready, take your attention and focus to your root chakra and then move through each chakra one at a time from the root to the crown. Connect to the dragon within it and be aware of their specific colours:

⫸ Root (bright clear ruby red)
⫸ Sacral (amber)
⫸ Navel (silver)
⫸ Solar plexus (vibrant gold)
⫸ Heart (translucent white)
⫸ Throat (aquamarine)
⫸ Third eye (lilac)
⫸ Crown (platinum)

With each chakra, ask yourself:

⫸ How does this chakra feel?
⫸ What is the dragon telling me?
⫸ What am I feeling and sensing about myself, my energy and the energy of the chakra?
⫸ Is there any healing to carry out? Ask the dragon to guide you.

CHAPTER

5

Dragons and Colour

Your dragons' colours are important. So when you connect with any of your dragons and you sense or see their colours make some notes on how your dragon feels to you and what feeling you get about its colours. Their colours can convey any healing work you need to carry out for yourself and information about your spiritual journey.

As I mentioned earlier, dragons frequently appear in two colours. Dual-coloured dragons have one colour running from the tip of their nose to the tip of their tail while the other colour runs from under their chin along their underside to the end of their tail. The tops and underneath their wings also carry the two colours.

This regularly raises the question: "What does this (or that) colour dragon mean?" The dragons have told me that when they show themselves in this way this indicates where your attention needs to focus. Your hidden or unconscious and spiritual self/mind is represented by the colour of the dragons' underside and your conscious/ physical self is represented by the colours along the top from their nose to the tail.

So, for example, if your dragon shows up with red underneath and blue on top, there are two aspects of yourself to work with and consider. Red is all about passion, desire, grounding, energy, resilience, anger and assertiveness. Blue is communication, spirituality, authority, bravery, independence and flow (think of bodies of water such the oceans).

Think about how these colours relate to you and your life and ask yourself these questions:

- What are you not grasping or acknowledging in your life right now that connects with the red aspect? Are you fully grounded, for example?
- Do you need to carry out any healing with the red (unconscious) aspect of your dragon? Are you carrying anger or frustration or do you become easily irritated and fly off the handle, for example?
- Do you need to be more grounded to reach your spiritual potential? Or are you passionate and full of energy?
- Which aspect of the blue energy do you need to recognize and work with consciously?
- Do you need to speak up more or learn to flow better?
- Do you need to be clearer in your communication with others?

None of these are fixed questions to think about – only suggestions and ideas for you to explore with your dragons. You can of course ask your dragon about their colour combination. They will always share their wisdom with you.

Your job is to be honest with yourself about how you feel and then acknowledge and accept that you are, like all of us, a work in progress. None of us are perfect and we are all always learning and growing spiritually and personally. Do you see how the shadow self creeps in here? The dragons are once again adept teachers in gaining our attention and directing it at where we need to be looking to heal and develop.

We humans often feel we frequently have to show the world we are something we are not. We need to feel accepted, appreciated, loved, recognized and acknowledged; this is all part of our human experience. So to fit that criteria we keep pretending until it becomes a part of who we are on the surface. But it is not a truth on a deeper authentic or heart level.

Follow your intuition and feelings and, as always, be completely honest with yourself. We are experts in kidding ourselves and believe the lies (yes, lies) that we tell ourselves. This can be hard to accept and work through but remember you are not walking this path alone. Your dragons are here to help, guide and support you every step of the way.

Colour Meanings

The list below contains the most common colours that show themselves with the dragons along with ideas for their colour meanings, with input from the dragons and my friend Andrea who works with colour. Remember that the dragons can be any colour combination and on occasions carry three colours. Do feel free to add your own thoughts, feelings and insights – colour is a pretty subjective topic and there are other colours as well.

Black: Space (think night sky), power, authority, serious, dramatic, expanse, velvet, creativity, mysterious – black also absorbs all the other colours

Blues: Communication, bravery, authority, emotions, spiritual growth, healing, flow, space (think sea and sky) sovereignty

Dark blue: Single-minded, tenacious, unbending

Light blue: Uplifting, faith, encouragement

Royal blue: Power, knowing your worth, owning your sovereignty, duty, spiritual, releasing, authenticity

Sky blue: Universal healer, calmness

Turquoise: Tranquil, sociable, immunity, communication

Brown: Earth, growth, stable, reliable and practical, moderate, common sense, down-to-earth

Gold: Wisdom, wealth, power, trust, authentic, confidence, royalty, forgiveness, soul experience, sovereignty

Greens: Healing, self-care, balance, nature, growth

Emerald: Healing, abundance, harmony

Pale green: New things, new experiences, compassion

Grey: Realism, respectable, soothing, calm

Indigo: Third eye, idealism, time and space, wisdom, psychic ability, devotion, higher knowledge

Lavender: Sensitive, elusive, soul star

Lilac: Emotional, caring, higher self, higher dimensional connection, strength, magical

Magenta: Transformation and change, uplifting, releasing of old patterns, letting go

Mauve: Intuition, spiritual, gentle healing, ideas, calm, majestic, peace

Orange: Creativity, warmth, uplifting, pushing through your comfort zone joy, social, warm-hearted, generous

Pink: Harmony, kindness, healing, love, affectionate, nurture, spiritual beauty, compassion

Purple: Spiritual connection, empowerment, wealth, majesty, ceremony and magic, royal, mystical, vision, dignified

Red: Energy, willpower, active, grounding, life force, passion, danger, anger, growth, perseverance

Violet: St Germain, transmutation and transformation, discernment, spirituality, higher connection, respect, dedication, intuition, destiny

White: Purity, openness, contains all the colours, unity

Yellow: Joy, laughter, discernment, honesty, courage, confidence, mental agility, tolerance

Dragon Colours Visualization

Begin with using the head and heart meditation in chapter one to ensure that you are grounded and present.

1. Form your dragon in your mind's eye. Starting at their feet get a sense of their size, scales, colouring and shape. Do they have long or short talons? What about their legs, neck and chest? Are they large and broad, or are they delicate and small?
2. What colour or colours do you sense and see? Focusing on the colours (or one colour at a time) what do you feel? Which sensations, thoughts and feelings flow through you?

3. Sit with your sensations, thoughts and feelings, allowing them to enter your senses, to flow over and through you.
4. When you feel this is complete, gently open your eyes and see how you feel.

This visualization can be repeated as frequently as you wish or when your dragons guide you to do it. As always, write down as much as you can recall in as much detail as you can as this will become your personal dragon colour library.

Solid One Colour Dragons

Some dragons are solid colours. These guys are unique and tend to be the Master Teachers, Grand Masters and Guardian Dragons.

The Guardian Dragons are usually grey, black, brown, dark green or dark blue. There is also the red dragon, who in my experience is Dr Usui and the founder and creator of the reiki healing practice, followed by Magdalene's Sapphire Ray Dragons and the Dragons of Light who are all white. These will all be covered in a later chapter.

DRAGON TIP

- ⫸ *SOLID ONE-COLOUR DRAGONS TEND TO BE MASTER TEACHERS.*
- ⫸ *YOUR DRAGONS' COLOURS MAY CHANGE AS YOU DEVELOP AND GROW.*

CHAPTER

6

Conversations with the Dragons

By now you will have discovered that it is incredibly useful to write up your dragon meditations, thoughts, observations and notes. Here, I invite you to take your journaling a step further with your dragons. I call it "conversations with dragons". This is also another dragon lesson in mindfulness, taking you into a heart connection.

Before embarking on this exercise it is a good idea to give yourself a few minutes to use the head and heart meditation from chapter one. This will help to clear your mind and settle you emotionally, mentally and energetically.

Journaling

Our minds and thoughts are on the go 24/7 and most of the time they go unnoticed. When we begin to meditate it is often our unconscious mind that comes to the fore. Suddenly we have asked our brains to be quiet and, hey presto, the mind (conscious and unconscious) has the playpark all to itself and can run riot!

If you find meditation difficult because your mind keeps wandering off in various directions, it can be helpful to use your journal before you settle down to meditate. Use it to mind dump – talking through your day, concerns, fears or joys on paper. Working in this way helps to clear your mind of the stuff that is floating about unnoticed and unheard in your unconscious and conscious mind.

Do not plan what you are going to say. Simply begin with the first thing that comes into your head. This may even be: "Boy, I feel stupid doing this, what is the point, I don't know what to write about, it's a total waste of time." It can be about absolutely anything and everything that is on your mind: the good the bad and the indifferent. It does not have to be spiritual in nature; it can be about everyday problems, worries and concerns. You can use the space to stamp, scream, shout and rant if you wish. Mind dumping and ranting on the page can be cathartic and healing. Writing down a problem you may be having and working on untangling it with the dragons can be incredibly useful. You will be surprised at the clarity that can follow it.

You can develop a practice of writing every single day or write as and when it feels right to. There are no limits on how much or how often you do it. It is your journal so do it your way! It does not matter whether or not you can spell, how good or bad your writing is; none of this is important to the dragons.

Use it to float ideas past yourself. You may have questions about your development, your dragons or your health, job or family, for example. You can write about all of this and more using your writing to seek guidance from your dragons.

I will add here that your journal is your private space to ramble so I would suggest that you do not share it with anyone unless you wish to do so. I frequently write longhand before transcribing to my computer so I have filled a huge number of journals over the years. These get left lying around the house but my husband would never dream of looking at any of them. These are my space to think. Much of this book has been written using my dragon journals.

Asking the Dragons for Help

As you have probably discovered, the dragons are straightforward and pragmatic. This of course makes them brilliant at helping us to untangle ourselves mentally, emotionally and spiritually. If you have a particular problem or question you are wrestling with, ask the dragons to help you with it, to find a solution, common ground, a way forward, etc. You will be surprised what practising this exercise can lead to.

When you begin this particular exercise you may find you feel you need to rewrite your question(s) a few times, getting the phrasing right. It does not necessarily mean that your question is wrong, but be prepared that it may not "feel" quite right as you try to understand more deeply what you are trying to express on paper. This is a great dragon lesson of learning to feel into things. It all takes time and practice. Making perceived mistakes helps you to discern where you can improve, grow and make changes.

You may prefer to make a list of questions. Again this is a great way to discover how you feel about what you are writing. Your dragon list may look something like this:

- ⫸ How do I learn to connect with you better?
- ⫸ What can I do about the state of the world?
- ⫸ Why can't I see you?
- ⫸ How can I help my friend, mum, dad, grandparents?
- ⫸ What do your colour(s) mean?
- ⫸ What is your role with me?
- ⫸ What can I do about this, that or the other at work?
- ⫸ What can I do about so-and-so at work?
- ⫸ How do I afford to get the car, oven, etc fixed?

Before you begin asking for your dragon's input and guidance, decide which question is the most pressing. Once you have settled on a particular one, observe yourself using the following steps.

1. Notice where your fear or self-doubt sits.
2. Notice how your body feels. Is there tension; if so, where? Is your jaw clenched? Is your tongue glued to your teeth or roof of your mouth? Are your shoulders tight?
3. Are you chasing worrying thoughts around your mind, like the swirling of a washing machine, going over and over the same cycle?

This doesn't give you *carte blanche* to go into self-flagellation or give yourself a hard time, but this is your opportunity to observe how or what you are feeling and thinking.

Let us use the first question on the list above as an example: How do I learn to connect with you better? What do I need to do? You may find this question requires a bit of jiggling around.

» What do I need to do to make a stronger connection to my dragon guides?
» What steps do I need to take to communicate more clearly with you?
» What I am missing in our communication?

As you are writing, ideas and thoughts will begin to flow or pop into your mind. But be careful you do not fall into the trap of overthinking and analysing what drops in or you run the risk of disappearing down various rabbit holes with your thoughts.

Be aware of what you feel. What is your dragon suggesting? What feelings are they imparting to you? Write it all down – every little nuance, feeling, idea, image or word that floats through your consciousness and body. Not all of it will be relevant, and over time you will begin to know the difference. It will take a bit of practice but once the flow starts there is no stopping it. And solutions can come in surprising ways.

Watch your thoughts with curiosity. What ideas are popping into your mind? Which ones bring a huge inner smile as you hit on the right one? They may feel like a click in your heart and consciousness. This is a frequent way in which the dragons interact with us. Thoughts float into your consciousness out of nowhere, it seems, and they are the perfect solution or stepping stone for us at the time.

If you find you are drawing a blank, that nothing is popping in and solutions are in short supply, simply keep writing your question. You may have to write it five, ten or more times before ideas begin to flow, a little like writing an affirmation.

There may be times when you will feel like nothing is happening. Know that your question has been heard and watch out for synchronicities. The dragons love to use the Universe to answer our pleas. Those little "coincidences" are a game changer! We often label them as odd or a little spooky! Your job here is to notice them and fully acknowledge them. Then it is up to you to follow them. At times it can be like following a trail of breadcrumbs while at other times you get the *Full Monty* show! Once you shift your focus, magic with the dragons really takes shape.

Talking with Your Dragons

You will have discovered that using your journal to communicate with your dragons can be extremely useful. With practice and over time you will enter into a full dialogue with them. Their help, support and advice can be pragmatic and straightforward. But I have a sneaking suspicion that you have already experienced their "no nonsense" approach.

On the next page is an example of some of my journaling with my dragons over the years.

DRAGON TALK

15 May

*"You don't trust yourself nor trust what
you get. We give you information; you need
to do it, write it or act upon it, only then
will you begin to build your trust in us
and you. Try it, you have nothing to lose,
but everything to gain. Your mother told
you this many times as a child."*

MM (Mother Mary is a Grand Master and is Serene in my deck)

She has an astonishingly tranquil energy
about her. She radiates peace and calm and
is a shepherdess of people (no idea what
that means). She had this to say:

*"I am the powerhouse of calm – great
achievements come about with a peaceful mind
and tranquil heart. I invite you to step
into the power to embrace it and own it.*

*"You can't change that which is done; you
must learn from it and move on – you can't
dwell. I encourage you to work for peace,
but that peace must begin with you. All the
time you have unrest in your heart, your
outer world will keep reflecting it back at
you until you shift dimensions. You must
crank it up a gear or two. Reflect love and
calmness and the world around you will
begin to shift.*

*"The colours of blue and yellow together,
blue for thought and communication, yellow*

for conscious thought and emotion. Together they make green, healing of all that surrounds you, including you. Wear the colours, surround yourself with them, and allow your psyche to absorb them, invite tranquillity in. Lift your vibration, your intent. Live it."

The following is a conversation I had with Solomon, one of my dragon guides. I must have decided to begin to write it down mid conversation!

3 July

CM: That really doesn't help my cause or notes, does it? Why was manifestation different then?

Solomon: *"The ancients used magik and not for personal gain, initially!"*

CM: So what was manifestation used for?

Solomon: *"Healing mainly. Understanding messages hidden in old text. Asking for illumination and it happening almost instantly."*

All this is sounding a bit weird and very like imagination, sci-fi stuff. I have learnt over the years to go with it, leave nothing out, and if it's right, all will become clear at a later date.

CM: So the illumination would be about what?

Solomon: *"Magic."*

Still none the wiser. I get it, as in I know it and feel it but can't explain it, which is the bugger of conversing with a dragon!

Solomon: *"There was very little illness in Atlantis. People would come to see the Magi or Mage and would be healed. They lived for an inordinately length of time. Broken bones healed overnight, severe burns gone with a day or two."*

CM: So back to manifestation. Ahh, get it. Manifestation was used for the greater good of all, not for personal gain.

Solomon: *"There was no need for wealth in Atlantis. Status was given by the powers you possessed as a healer and the accuracy of your insights. Although in reality, there still was no status."*

CM: So it was the beginnings of communism then, except in an advanced way.

Solomon: *"You could look at it that way in effect. Although it is not fully accurate nor is it the full picture."*

I still do not fully understand, but I will leave that one to simmer a little longer.

DRAGON TIP

- *ALWAYS DATE YOUR PAGE SO YOU CAN PLOT YOUR PROGRESS AND SEE HOW MUCH YOU HAVE LEARNT AND GROWN.*

- *YOU MAY FIND IT USEFUL TO MIND DUMP (AS I THINK OF MY JOURNALS) BEFORE MEDITATING, ESPECIALLY IF YOU ARE THE TYPE OF PERSON WHOSE MIND IS CONSTANTLY JUMPING AROUND WITH THOUGHTS CRASHING AND BUMPING INTO EACH OTHER, GOING OFF ON TANGENTS.*

CHAPTER

7

The Grand Masters

If you have my deck, the Dragon Path Oracle cards, you will be familiar with the dragon clan of the Grand Masters (GMs). The Grand Masters are the master spiritual teachers of the dragon world. When they first introduced themselves to me I was a bit flummoxed by the fact that they could shapeshift. They were known for a long time as the shapeshifters until they informed me in such a way as only dragons can: "We are known as the Grand Masters."

So what makes a dragon a Grand Master? A Grand Master has the ability to present as either a human form (and occasionally angelic form) or dragon form. The dragon side of a Grand Master tends to be more direct and forthright (they certainly pack a punch energetically) whereas their other human side tends to be gentler most of the time. Their human image is that of a highly evolved spiritual teacher. These are usually Ascended Masters (AMs).

In my deck we have Mother Mary, whose dragon counterpart is that of Serene, and then there is Merlin the Dragon and Merlin the Magician, so you get the picture. We also have Illuminare; his other side is that of the archangel Uriel. This did throw me into a bit of spin – I will talk more about him in a minute.

What is interesting with the Ascended Masters is that not all of them chose to have a dragon counterpart. I have no idea why this should be but it is certainly how it appears. The other point here is there were a few other Ascended Masters who were also Grand Masters but refused to be in the deck. One memorable one is Mary Magdalene. I was desperate to have Mary Magdalene in my deck, but, boy, she is a tough cookie and totally refused. We had numerable conversations but she still would not budge.

Other Ascended Masters who can shapeshift are Jesus, Archangel Michael and Metatron. These are not the only ones and you will discover your own as you walk along this path. Do not be surprised once you begin to work with them if they swap from shape to shape. One day being a Grand Master and the next showing up as an Ascended Master. Both forms will have a lot to teach you of a spiritual nature.

Grand Masters and Their Roles

The following dragons are not exhaustive, but this gives you a flavour of some of the common Grand Masters, their roles and how to work with them.

Illuminare/Uriel

Illuminare was one of my surprise Grand Masters.

In October 2016 I was out walking and was joined by the archangel Uriel. He guided me to stop at a particular spot along the woodland track and to stand within the centre of a sunbeam that would be coming through the trees. I stopped when guided to and I was instructed to stand quietly still, watch and listen.

So I stood, watched, felt and listened. I became still and peacefully quiet. I watched as all around me the autumn leaves fell like coloured snowflakes of yellow, bronze, gold and red, floating their way gently to Earth. I observed the leaves that remained. They were determinedly hanging in place as the breeze lifted and fluttered them, as if they were not yet ready to say goodbye to their home in the early autumn sunshine.

All was calm and quiet and I felt cocooned in a bubble of light held within my sunbeam as I stood among the great trees of oak and beech. Suddenly, externally, everything stilled and quietened. I had asked for proof that Uriel was there and it came in the form of complete stillness. No sound or movement until he guided me to look upwards as one golden leaf spiralled down through my sunbeam, landing noiselessly at my feet.

It was shortly after this that Uriel informed me he had a counterpart, that of the dragon Illuminare. The fact that Illuminare is Uriel and Uriel is Illuminare threw me into a bit of spin because in my mind the angels were angels and dragons were dragons.

What I now understand is that all spiritual beings will collaborate and work with others in any way that will serve and guide us humans. Isn't that beautiful? We humans with our fixed ideas and prejudices create the issue.

Illuminare went on to tell me that he shows us "that which is hidden yet illuminates all that is". I had to spend quite a bit more time with Illuminare to understand his full message for my dragon deck.

In Doreen Virtues' book *Archangels and Ascended Masters* she says this about Uriel:

"Uriel's name means 'God is light', 'God's light' or 'fire of God' because he illuminates situations ..."

Here is a perfect example of the dragons talking to us via the Universe. Illuminare needed me to make the connection between him and Uriel. Uriel needed me to be still and peaceful to get his message across and used the beautiful autumn sunlight. There could not have been a more perfect way to do it, using the beautiful rays of sunbeams and being with the natural world.

If you are seeking answers, call on Illuminare; let him be your guide, to light your way forward. And to connect with Uriel outside in nature is as good a place as any.

A Walking Meditation to Connect with Uriel/Illuminare

A walking meditation is quite different from being indoors and still. It may take a little practice so please be gentle with yourself as you discover this way of being with yourself outside.

Firstly decide where you want to walk, whether this is a river bank, mountain range, beach, formal gardens, woodland area, your local park ... and do ensure you are dressed for the terrain and the weather! A charged mobile phone is always a good idea, even if only to capture some inspiring images from your explorations outside in nature. You may like to put it on silent mode when you begin your walk though. It may also be worth, if you can, taking a notebook and pen with you and some water. Once you begin walking you could find yourself out and about for a while.

During your walk you may find yourself being drawn to stop and sit down to write or draw. Follow those feelings, senses and inner knowing. Do not think about it or start second guessing yourself. You will tie yourself in knots and defeat the object of being present outside in nature and the natural world and you will close off the connection you are trying to make.

With all the things the dragons have taught me, this exercise is incredibly simple, so do not over complicate things with your thinking mind. Before setting off for your walk set your intention either silently or out loud. You can of course write it in your dragon journal/notebook.

It could go something like this:

"Uriel (or Illuminare) please guide me in my walk to connect with you more deeply/for the first time."

Or:

"Illuminare (or Uriel) please step forward during my walk. I welcome your guidance on/with [add what you would like some dragon support with]."

Now you are all set to go.

1. Once you begin walking, notice your posture. Are you walking with your head down looking at the ground? Are you wearing your shoulders as earrings? Or is your back straight with your shoulders drawn comfortably back and down? If not, consciously shift your posture, taking a deep slow breath in, relaxing and dropping your shoulders back and down and lifting your head. Are your hands in your pockets? If they are, remove them from your pockets. Or are they hanging loose and comfortable by your sides, moving gently with each stride? These are only little things but they make a world of difference to your walking and how you feel. Make some adjustments to your posture. Then spend a few minutes walking in this way, noticing when you begin to slouch or drop your head.
2. Now you have some awareness of your physical body, take your attention to your thoughts. What are they doing? Are you irritated that you can't walk with your hands in your pockets? Or do you habitually keep looking at the ground? Is your mind on the long list of chores you need to do at work, home, with the kids, parents and so on? Do not go into judgement here; just quietly observe your physical body and your thoughts.

3. Once you have done this for a few more minutes, take your full attention to your feet and the Earth. Feel each step, each heel toe connection to the Earth as you walk. Feel the earth, sand, stones through your shoes. Feel and sense your connection to Gaia, our home and the Earth. You can of course walk barefoot too, if you wish. Gradually your other senses and awareness will expand. Remember to stay with your awareness on each step. Here you will find your breathing will naturally regulate too. Walk at a pace that is comfortable for you.

4. Fall into a rhythm with your walking. This could take five minutes or 50 minutes. It does not matter how long but just remember to be gentle with yourself throughout this process. Your awareness continues to expand so feel for any guidance that floats into your mind. You may feel guided to stop and sit under a tree or pick up a pebble to watch a butterfly; any manner of things could happen. Follow your intuition and inner knowing, allowing it all to flow and float through and around you.

Here you may like to restate your question, but remember to keep a soft focus on each step you take. Have an awareness of the ground beneath your feet; otherwise you run the risk of going straight back into your thinking mind.

You may find yourself in full conversation with Illuminare. Allow it all to take place and remember the dragons will use the world around you to send you messages.

This all takes a bit of practice. If it seems like nothing much happened, keep an open mind and eye out for synchronicities over the coming days. Dragons are the most magical of beings!

This type of walking meditation can be used to connect with any of your dragons. Most of all enjoy the freedom of walking with them.

Platinum/St Germain

Platinum introduced me to the new chakra colours and how to work with them. The new chakra colours are a higher frequency (we shift from vibration to frequency with the dragons), which allows us to carry more light. This in turn accentuates our darker shadow side offering us an opportunity to grow and heal.

If the shadow self is new to you, this is the part of you that you like to ignore and pretend you do not have, such as anger, irritation, fear, jealousy, greed, guilt, stress, anxiety; all those "low vibrational things that are not love 'n' light". Sorry, folks, the dragons will not allow you to hide there now. We are in times of exponential growth, light and opportunity.

The shadow is a part of us that requires understanding, forgiveness, healing, compassion and acceptance. It is often wounded and involves things we all need to look at, accept, work on and heal where necessary. The more light we carry within ourselves and shine out into the Universe, the deeper the shadows are thrown, and it affects every part of Earth and our collective existence.

As more of us work on healing our shadow side and carrying more light, the more we support ourselves, the planet and the rest of humanity. This is the ripple effect, the macro and microcosm, and it is all perfect. It is all as it should and needs to be.

We are the spiritual warriors of Earth; this is why you have this book in your hands. You are ready to pick up the challenge and be part of the change the entire world needs right now. You are part of the solution not the problem.

Below is an example of working with your shadow side that Platinum took me through a few years ago. On that particular occasion he worked with a golden dragon, which I have not seen since.

My Platinum Experience

I was guided to go into meditation with the intention of carrying out some healing and clearing work around my heart chakra based around fear.

As I sat with the energy I could feel it build. I could sense the fear with every ounce of my being. I felt I needed to sit with it, not to interact with it but to watch and observe. As I did this the fear grew and grew and then without warning began to morph. It shifted shape and steadily moved through fear, guilt, hatred (that really shocked me!) and anger until it eventually settled at a white hot fury before moving into hatred.

As I sat with each of these feelings, watching and observing them, vaguely wondering "what the Dickens is going on and what am I supposed to do now" (I was also still reeling from the shock that I could feel fury and hatred so violently and passionately), two incredibly beautiful dragons came into my awareness. One was Platinum Dragon and the other was a gold dragon.

Platinum went to work on removing the fear. He began to fill my heart chakra with silver light. This fear was so entrenched in my way of being that it took some time. He had to wiggle it around the edges, to fill the tiny gaps and cracks around the edge of my heart. Gradually my heart filled with silver light and he was able to lift away a heavy, dark and deep cone shape that had been lodged there. I felt (and still to this day, feel) physically lighter in my heart chakra.

The gold dragon came in to clear the hatred and fury. This was actually far less intense as these are rarely emotions I feel but were obviously still present in my energy field.

That was quite an experience! After this particular episode, Platinum Dragon began to nag me about working with the violet flame.

This actually took a bit longer than planned, but as ever the dragons, Universe and synchronicity all kicked in eventually a few years later when a client brought myself and an old friend of mine, Tracy, back together. Tracy had been living in South

Africa and we had lost touch. The dragons wanted me to do my violet flame attunement with Tracy so I had to wait to be reconnected with her. And of course it was perfect!

Sometimes with the dragons all the dots get joined up so quickly that it makes your head spin, and other times it can take literally years. It is always about timing and being ready to take those steps when they appear.

Both Platinum and St Germain (and the violet flame) encourage us to carry clear bright energy. This includes our auric field and our chakras.

If you do not have time to carry out a full aura and chakra cleanse with Platinum, this little decree written by Elizabeth Clare Prophet (taken from her book *Violet Flame to Heal Mind, Body and Soul*) is a fantastic way to burn off unwanted energies, cords and any other detritus we manage to pick up energetically in our day to day lives.

Decree – Tube of Light

Beloved I AM Presence bright
Round me seal your tube of light
From Ascended Master flame
Called forth now in God's own Name.
Let it keep my temple free
From all discord sent to me.

I AM calling forth violet fire
To blaze and transmute all desire,
Keeping on in Freedoms' name
Till I AM one with the violet flame.
(repeat three times)

Platinum also taught me that our aura and chakras are part of our light body. I cover this in more detail in chapter 13.

Below are couple of meditations for you to experience. The first one is a chakra clearing with Platinum. Take your time with this one and use it as frequently as you wish. Each time you practise it will most likely be different.

We can carry lifetimes of pain, trauma and other emotions within our energy system. Once your spiritual and, in particular, your healing journey begins, you gradually uncover more work to do as your understanding deepens. And there will be times where you become exasperated and frustrated, especially if repeat "old self-clutter" keeps coming up to be cleared. There is a saying that healing, in particular emotions or emotional pain healing, is akin to the layers of an onion skin. You just keep peeling it away one a layer at a time.

I believe we heal at a level we are able to understand at any given moment, and our understanding and knowledge grows as our spiritual awareness deepens, as does our ability to heal.

On top of the past life pain, trauma and memories held within our energy system, we also have the day to day energetic garbage we pick up too. The person crying in the staff canteen, a falling out with a friend, the image you saw on social media – all of these things and more affect your energetic makeup. In short, your energetic system needs a good spring clean as a minimum and ideally a shower at least once or twice a week. It is good practice and housekeeping to keep a clear energetic system and carry out one of these exercises regularly. You can use the violet flame decree or the full chakra clearing meditation.

The second meditation is a meditation with Platinum in the Great Temple in Atlantis. It gives you the opportunity to experience a partial or total chakra upgrade. As a side note, Platinum Dragon is one of 12 dragons that held a place within the great Atlantean temple. If you have a connection with Atlantis, Platinum is the dragon you need. He will be your guide and teacher for everything Atlantean related.

Before embarking on either of the exercises below, give yourself a few minutes to use the head and heart meditation from chapter one to settle yourself into your dragon working space.

Chakra Clearing Meditation

Below are two different meditations, both of which are options for a chakra energy upgrade.

Have a read of them both and work with the one which suits your needs now.

Settle yourself in your usual meditation spot. Once you are ready, carry out a mental scan of each of your chakras in turn, starting at the root, followed by your sacral, navel, solar plexus, heart, throat, third eye and crown. Feel into each one, observing and sensing for blocks, sluggish energy, anything that feels a little off kilter or out of balance.

Each time, ask yourself:

1. Does the colour feel right?
2. Is it bright or dull in colour?
3. Is it spinning? If so, which way – clockwise or anti clockwise?
4. Does it feel fast or slow?
5. What are you sensing about it?

Take your time as you work through each chakra in turn asking Platinum Dragon to join you to clear any blocks or stuck energy you may have. Once you have completed this, Platinum steps forward and asks if you are ready for your chakra upgrade. Are you ready to clear old patterns and ways of being from your life? Are you ready to change and make changes? If you are, give him one clear nod of your head. As he breathes the violet flame energy into each chakra, feel for any shifts or changes that take place. Be aware of emotions surfacing. What are they? Observe them.

1. Platinum gently breathes silver/violet fire into your root chakra. How does it feel and what do you notice?
2. Platinum gently breathes silver/violet fire into your sacral chakra. How does it feel and what do you notice?
3. Platinum gently breathes silver/violet fire into your navel chakra. How does it feel and what do you notice?
4. Platinum gently breathes silver/violet fire into your solar plexus chakra. How does it feel and what do you notice?
5. Platinum gently breathes silver/violet fire into your heart chakra. How does it feel and what do you notice?
6. Platinum gently breathes silver/violet fire into your throat chakra. How does it feel and what do you notice?
7. Platinum gently breathes silver/violet fire into your third eye chakra. How does it feel and what do you notice?
8. Platinum gently breathes silver/violet fire into your crown chakra. How does it feel and what do you notice?

Before you finish, ask Platinum about the work you have completed together, what it means for you and what else you can do to deepen your spiritual growth and healing. The dragons will always be your best guides.

Before closing down, give yourself a few minutes to feel into your now clear energy, seeing what feels different and how you feel different.

Once you are finished, remember to close your chakras from your crown to your root and of course write up your experiences.

Chakra Upgrade with Platinum

I brought up the topic of new chakra colours in chapter four with the Dragons and the Chakras section. Here we delve a little deeper into these chakras. But first of all, here is a quick colour recap.

Traditional colour	**New colour**
Root – Red	Root – Bright clear ruby red
Sacral – Orange	Sacral – Amber
Navel – (No clear colour)	Navel – Silver
Solar Plexus – Yellow	Solar Plexus – Bright gold
Heart – Pink/green	Heart – White
Throat – Pale/light blue	Throat – Aquamarine
Third Eye – Indigo	Third Eye – Lilac
Crown – Purple	Crown – Platinum

The colours have not changed massively but what they have done is altered in frequency, i.e. the amount of light they are able to carry.

Energy Upgrade with Platinum Dragon

Settle yourself in your usual way in your meditation space, using the head and heart meditation from chapter one.

1. In your mind's eye vizualize yourself walking through a narrow bustling street of Atlantis following the flow of people. As you are walking you notice the light is different; it somehow shimmers and moves, but as soon as you focus on it, it is gone. Everything is bathed in a warm pale glow: the buildings, the cobbles on the streets. You try to work out if it is actually the light or the fabric of the buildings themselves.

2. Eventually the narrow street opens up into a large plaza. It is warm and vibrant. There are street traders selling food, coloured silk fabrics, all manner of things, and the buildings carry a warm golden glow. You spend some time walking around the market, taking in the sights, smells and sounds.

3. Your attention is drawn to a set of shallow steps off to one side of the plaza, leading to the Great Temple of Atlantis. You know this is why you have come and now it is time. You walk up the 11 steps and across the large open terrace to a pair of huge, ornately carved oak doors that reach from floor to ceiling. Considering their size, the doors move easily and smoothly as you push against them and they swing effortlessly inward. The air inside is cool and your eyes take a little while to adjust to the dim light. You can smell the burning incense; it is familiar to you, you know it at the core of your being. Slowly the cavernous room comes into focus and you are drawn forward as if by an invisible cord.

4. You are gently being pulled toward a raised circular platform with three shallow steps running all the way

around it so that it can be accessed from any direction. Along the outside edge there are 24 beautifully carved stone pillars. At the base of each stone pillar a line is carved into the stone floor crossing the dais to the pillar exactly opposite. Each of the pillars is connected to its opposite number. At the centre a stunning golden starburst shape is created where all the lines meet and cross each other.

5. As you approach, the pillars begin to shimmer and the light appears to bounce off them. You are guided toward the centre of the golden starburst. There you find huge scatter cushions and a circle of small glowing candles. You take your place on the cushions, wondering what is going to happen next as you feel the energy of the starburst beneath you.

6. Your attention is still drawn by the shimmering pillars. As you watch, a dragon begins to form from one of them. This is Platinum Dragon, a Grand Master of Atlantis, his human counterpart being St Germain of the violet flame.

7. He steps toward you, his chakra colours glowing brightly in the dim light of the temple. He asks you to stand and as you do so he breathes his violet flames over you. It is surprisingly cool and the colours vary from pale lilac to purple to ultraviolet.

8. His violet flame burns away everything you have been holding on to, everything that no longer serves you as a being of light and spiritual warrior. Everything and anything that is held within your auric field is being cleared and removed. Outdated beliefs that no longer serve you and your highest potential disperse and transmute. Fears, insecurities, anger, jealously, doubts and more transform under the blaze of violet fire.

9. Spend as much time as you feel you need to complete your work with Platinum. He will adjust your chakras as is right for you at this time, bathing you in the right frequency of light. He will work with you to clear and cleanse on any and every level you choose.

Dragons and Atlantis

There is much magic and mystery surrounding Atlantis and just as many theories and ideas. Atlantis was certainly a far more highly evolved planet than we currently live in. The dragons gave me a whopping download about Atlantis, some of which is transcribed below.

The dragons (in particular the Galactic Dragons) were actively involved in the birthing and creation of Atlantis (just like they did with Lemuria and our planet) physically, energetically and spiritually. It was information from the Galactic Dragons that made Atlantis the evolved and advanced society it was. I also have a really strong feeling (a knowing) that there is a connection and correlation between ancient Egypt and Atlantis.

ATLANTIS AND THE DRAGONS

If Atlantis is a new concept to you, here is a little background given to me by what I initially thought was a dragon.

"In short, Atlantis is in a different dimension to this one, the one we inhabit today. There are many galaxies within our multi-universe, with all the planets, constellations, black holes, etc. Dimensions on the other hand are beyond our Universe.

"Atlantis, Lemuria, the Acturians and others are interdimensional beings (Acturians are star beings, sometimes known as light beings) and have their home beyond our own galactic Universe. The Pleiades too are of another dimension, yet they, like the Acturians, have localized satellite stations within our galaxy."

The light being who passed me this information was in fact a higher dimensional light being from Sirius. I asked him to fill in my gaps of the Pleiades, Atlantis, the dragons and the galactic connections.

In short, to connect with these beings of light (Sirius, Pleiades, Andromeda and others) our vibration requires lifting and lightening. I have since learnt that we require a frequency upgrade(!) to communicate fully and have a stable connection. I liken this to having super-fast broadband rather than the old dial-up system. Our light bodies need reawakening and our personal matrix requires realigning or repairing.

Sirius went on to say that others can't and should not do this work for you. It is your personal energy system and another being should not interfere with it. You can be taught or guided but you must do the work yourself.

So to get the most out of our work with the dragons and the light beings, like those of Atlantis, Lemuria and others, we need to lift our energy and our own light body matrix. What a journey!

There are two entire chapters in this book dedicated to working with your personal light matrix (chapter 14) and those of the planet (chapter 12).

The Temple Guardians

There were 12 Guardians of Atlantis – six male and six female. Their role was to guide the seers (the dragons tell me the seers were actually blind) and the dragons were greatly revered holding high status within the echelons of Atlantis. The 12 Guardians have shown themselves to me a couple of times over the years, one at what is known as the Table of the Gods and the other at the Great Temple of Atlantis. They had this to say about their lives and work:

DRAGON TALK

"We are the Council of Twelve; Twelve Grand Masters and Twelve Ascended Masters. We sit at the Great Table together, each AM has a dragon counterpart which stands behind them. We used to protect the Temple of Atlantis, one pillar for each, twenty four in total."

Many of the Ascended Masters we know and work with today had a lifetime in Atlantis – but of course they were not known by the names that we use to refer to them today. I suppose more accurately their energetic blueprint was present in Atlantis during that time. Many of them carried the knowledge they had in Atlantis out into the world in subsequent incarnations, hence them being the Wise Ones.

Within Atlantis there was what was known as the "Great Temple" – this is where all major decisions were made, where magic was practised and where dragons and the Ascended Masters resided. Within the temple there was a vast raised central circle with three steps going up to it. Within the central circle there were 24 pillars: 12 were dragon and 12 were the Wise Ones. Both dragon and human could blend together and morph into pillars unseen by the uninitiated.

The Temple Guardians consisted of six female and six male Ascended Masters. Below are the Ascended Masters with their dragon counterparts.

- Mother Mary – Serene
- Lady Portia – Justice

- Mary Magdalene – Kindness
- Sekhmet – Healing
- Lilith – Power
- Artemis – Purity
- Merlin – Merlin the Dragon
- Metatron – Metatron the Dragon
- Melchizedek – Melchizedek the Dragon
- Thoth – The Scribe
- St Germain – Platinum
- Archangel Michael – Unity

You can invite any of the Ascended Masters to support and guide you. They may show up in either their dragon or human form. You can of course ask if you wish to connect with them as specifically a dragon or master. From an energy perspective there are subtle differences between the two. Both forms are powerful, wise and open hearted although I feel the dragon's energy of each Master carries a deeper and slightly more powerful edge: that gentle yet no nonsense energy that all the dragons carry.

The Collapse of Atlantis

I was also given the following information about Atlantis and its subsequent collapse. The dragons were the Guardians of Atlantis, guides to the seers of the time. Their job was to protect and guide the Holy Ones as the seers were known.

It was the seers' job to guide the priests and priestesses of Atlantis. The dragons were the protectors and guides to them all and were honoured and revered. They carried great wisdom and compassion much like they do today for us.

Over time a darkened energy began to creep into the society of Atlantis. Mistrust grew among all folk and spread like dark glue, slowly creeping and feeling its way. Long before this the dragons forewarned the seers that dark days were coming. They warned that fear, mistrust and discord would creep through their beautiful society causing conflict and arguments. If it was not halted it would become irreversible.

The seers passed this information to the priests and priestesses urging them to act. It went unheeded, eventually leading to the seers being scorned and rebutted. They lost their standing and reverence within the hierarchy. The dragons were tossed out; some were incarcered and chained within the dungeons of Atlantis, some fled and others were slain.

At this point the dark forces of Atlantis forbade the dragons from becoming involved with the life, prosperity and development of mankind. Due to the universal rules, the dragons could not interfere and everything had to take its course. They could only come to our aid if invited by other higher beings and at a time of human crisis. This of course took place in September 2001.

The dragons are the wisdom keepers of Atlantis in the same way we see the dolphins and in particular the whales as being the wisdom keepers of our planet.

Dr Usui

Usui was another curveball that the dragons threw me and another one that took a while to sort out. During my reiki training, a red dragon appeared at the beginning of the day. I did not take a great deal of notice as he was just a presence with us. But over the following months everyone I came into contact with who was clairvoyant kept giving me this red dragon. Every time it was mentioned I rolled my eyes and said it was not one of mine.

A long time later it all fell into place and I understood that the red dragon is Dr Usui, the founder of modern reiki. He had appeared that day to oversee what was taking place and stayed with me until I understood the message. So Dr Usui in either dragon form or human form can be called upon during a reiki healing or training to guide students, teachers and healers.

DRAGON TALK

Dragon Usui has this to say about energy healing:

"Children of Earth, everything around you vibrates. Everything has a frequency. Healing in simple terms is a frequency which alters the state of the human body. The frequency presented to the recipient is one of perfection, allowing the human body, mind, psyche, emotions and spirituality to find their natural equilibrium."

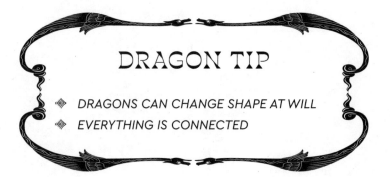

DRAGON TIP

> *DRAGONS CAN CHANGE SHAPE AT WILL*
> *EVERYTHING IS CONNECTED*

Part
Two

SPIRITUAL
WARRIORS OF EARTH

In part two, we begin working with frequency and
a whole new set of energy and dragons.

All of the dragons and work covered in the following
chapters encompass holding, activating and
anchoring new frequencies, light codes, personal
and planetary DNA coding for our collective
spiritual evolution and advancement.

We are asked to anchor the light into the world
wherever we are and send it out with no attachment
to outcome or agenda.

CHAPTER

8

Dragons of the Land

The Dragons of the Land consist of two separate clans:

⁂ Guardians of the Land and Sacred Sites
⁂ Earth Dragons

We are asked to treat all of Earth as ancient and sacred. Therefore Dragons of the Land are found in all kinds of places. They have two functions: some are the protectors of our sacred sites across the world while others are protectors of the land.

I have known for a number of years that a group of dragons connects to our ancient and Celtic lands here in the UK. I have also felt that they have a connection and kinship to the clans across the globe to other places and sites such as Machu Picchu, Sedona, Mount Shasta, Mount Saini, the Pyramids, the Vatican, Table Mountain, Uluru and others. These dragons are the Guardians of the Land and Sacred Sites, but their task actually carries a deeper meaning – that of keeping the energy lines clear.

A few years ago I was somewhat surprised to connect to a dragon in my garden. I asked her if she was the guardian of my home. She scoffed slightly at this idea, telling me that I was not actually that important! She is the guardian of the land that surrounds my home. We live opposite an old forest. The field behind us at one time was home to ancient burial mounds that are no longer visible.

The dragon within my garden is of the land. She keeps a watchful eye and protects the space around me and the land in which I live. But she is not mine. She belongs to the natural world. This is the same for the dragons I encountered whilst driving to Bath.

One particular December, my husband and I were travelling to Bath to help a friend celebrate a big birthday. As we were driving through the Wiltshire landscape, I was looking at the hills and valleys of the countryside we were passing through and announced to him, "There be dragons under them there hills." I now know these to be Earth Dragons. My husband duly rolled his eyes at me and continued driving without comment. But I could feel their presence; I could sense them and their energy, much in the same way I did when I met the Divine Feminine Dragon at Beacon Hill in West Berkshire.

Frequently it is the Earth Dragons that we encounter as slumbering or sleeping dragons. If you encounter a sleeping Earth Dragon, tune into their energy. Check in with them to feel if they need any healing or whether they are literally simply sleeping.

Follow your inner guidance at a heart level and intuition as to whether they should be woken. These dragons can become guides, teachers, healing dragons and more. If you feel it is time to wake them, do so gently by connecting with them and their energy. You may like to gently stroke them at first or shake them gently awake. Another way to begin awakening the Earth Dragons is by quietly drumming, using a regular rhythm and beat like that of the heartbeat of Mother Earth.

Spend some time and get to know the dragons in your area. Work outside in nature with them and allow them to guide you. Not all of the Earth Dragons will have a specific task of becoming a teacher or guide as this is not required of them. They can simply be a presence for us to connect with if we require it. They carry the wisdom and history of the place within the fabric of their being and will share it with us if we ask them to.

In many ways, the Earth Dragons are like our physical whales, the record keepers of Earth. The sites built and maintained by our ancestors carry our human story and history; we have much to learn from these places and the dragons that care for them.

When it comes to sacred sites the dragons do have specific roles. Below are some of the dragons I have encountered over the years.

Avebury Dragons

There is a pair of dragons within the surrounding landscape of Avebury. You have already met the Avebury Matriarch. Her male counterpart was a bit of a surprise. I encountered him under Silbury Hill. He had been incarcerated eons ago and was not a happy chap. My initial feeling to free him swiftly changed gear to one of connection; it took weeks of connecting to his energy every time I was there, sending healing and checking in on him.

One Samhain I had arranged to hook up with a coven who was visiting from Essex. Around 50 of us stood as close as we could get to Silbury Hill sending healing and light to this energetically wounded being. I could feel he was chained around his body and neck with a large stake piercing his tail. He had every right to be furious.

Once we had finished we all made our way up to the West Kennet Long Barrow. As we slipped and slid our way back down toward the road I was chatting to a couple of the ladies and they asked what the dragon's name was. I had no idea (as you know, dragons and names are not really a thing) so nonchalantly I said, "I know him only as Silbury Dragon." At that point I heard a booming voice ricochet across the landscape saying, "I AM THE GUARDIAN OF AVEBURY."

He was my first proper introduction to the Guardians of the Sacred Sites. Both Layla (who had brought the group down from Essex) and I continued to work with and send healing to the Guardian of Avebury. In the early spring of the following year we reconnected and released him from his chains. His tail now carries quite a magnificent scar of gold in the shape of a slightly wonky cross.

He is now rarely found at Silbury. One particular afternoon I was walking from the Tolkien Trees along the ramparts at Avebury Stone Circle wondering how he was doing and felt him swoosh up behind me. He was relishing in his newfound freedom, playing in the air.

He and the Avebury Matriarch have since taught me that they are an aspect of the divine masculine and divine feminine. Their joint role is to protect the site of Avebury, to keep and bring balance to the ancient temple and the energy around it.

Dragon of the Tor

I had known for some years that there was a dragon at the Tor in Glastonbury. (There are in fact two dragons at the Tor.) Over the years I had carried out a number of attempts to climb the Tor and connect with her, but for one reason or another my idea was always thwarted and I stopped short of completing the task. All very frustrating in my humanness!

Eventually one glorious late autumn day I knew it was time. The dragon had been calling to me for a couple of weeks but there was no time in my schedule to take the journey. Then one Saturday I cleared my diary, left my husband on dog duty and took off to Glastonbury. The following is what transpired that day.

The Guardian of the Tor is mighty and gentle. She carries the song of the dragon along the invisible energy lines that form around our planet. She battles to keep them clear and clean so beauty, love and compassion can flow freely through them without hindrance. And yet we come along with our pain, our frustration and anger and grief at the injustices and unfairness of the world and she carries that pain for us too.

Over time the song lines of Earth have become clogged with our wailing and wringing of our hands and our pain. The dragons continue to sing to clear our dross and drama, our selfish acts of overconcentration on the self and perceived injustices.

The dragons of our land, our planet, are tired. She is tired. They are the guardians of our Earth and the song lines which carry the invisible flow. Weaving the great web of light around the planet. They are our protectors of our sacred ancient sites.

Once upon a time these places were approached with reverence and respect but now they have become the playground for many and a dumping ground of emotional baggage for others. Not intentionally, of course. It is just the way we and the world have evolved and many have forgotten the sacredness of the space. Even many more have little or no understanding. And this is why we do have the understanding.

The Guardian of the Tor asks us respectfully to approach these sites with reverence and peace in our hearts. Of course many of these sites are a place of healing; this is why so many are drawn to them. Those of us who can are asked to support the dragons in maintaining the clarity of the energy of the sites and the dragon song lines.

The collective Guardians are asking for our help as individuals and groups to approach these landscapes with the intention of giving back, rebalancing and healing. For our intention to give unconditionally to the song lines that carry messages across the world. Messages of healing, hope and respect but above all gentleness. I talk more about this in the final chapter.

They ask of us: *To hold yourself gently, to approach others with gentle joy and openness, to embrace it all.*

The Guardian of the Tor asks that we support her and all the land guardians in healing the song lines for this is how our story is carried. The energy we leave in the land is carried along these invisible, yet powerful strings of light. It does not transmute or transform; it is simply carried along on the tide of energy.

St. Catherine's Hill, Winchester

I have been being drawn to St Catherine's Hill in Winchester for some time. At the Summer Solstice of 2019 the dragons told me that I was to begin to walk the wheel of the year starting at Samhain. I finally took heed of their word and began to honour the turning of the year at Samhain in 2020. This took the form of walking the labyrinth on top of St Catherine's Hill.

It was not until early November 2021 that I connected with the dragon who resides there. On a previous visit I had found one of the leys there and my intention had been to follow its course. Interestingly that day the ley was not easy to find – it felt like it kept disappearing – so I decided to leave it for another time and walked the labyrinth instead. That was also challenging and my balance was off as I traversed the turns. It was all food for thought and led to deeper contemplation.

Once I arrived at the centre I was guided to be still and connect with the land more deeply. As I did so I felt the female dragon come to greet me. She is the same blue as the Guardian of the Tor. She gently snaked her head up my leg, settling at my hip. It was a beautiful experience.

Every place has a different feel to it, which is why if you can visit them in person you should do so. There is much to learn and experience by taking these trips. St Catherine's Hill does not have the sacred feel to it that I experienced at the Tor or Avebury, but then the land was once an Iron Age Fort and has been split in half with a motorway running through it.

The dragon who resides there is a beautiful being and enjoys her connection with humans. She is the Guardian of the Land there but not many know of her. Approach the site with an open heart and she will come to greet you.

Stonehenge

When I was a child, my parents used to take me to Stonehenge before it was taken over by English Heritage (and closed off in terms of having open access to it) as a monument of historical interest. Before this we could walk among the stones, feel them, touch them and connect to the Earth.

I have felt for a number of years that the land there has no energy. It feels flat like there is nothing there and this is echoed by others I have spoken to. There could be a number of reasons for this.

During the 1960s many of the stones were concreted in place as they were unstable. This may have a bearing on the lack of energy there. Another consideration is that the land is no longer used as it was meant to be except at the mid-winter and summer solstices, and then that is just for many to party. It is like the dragons and the energy have retreated.

Some years ago shortly before the spring equinox, I had been invited to work with another lady to carry out some work balancing the divine masculine and divine feminine of Stonehenge. Of course anything I am involved in always brings in dragon energy, and I felt that Galactic Dragons preside over the site. The role of Galactic Dragons with Stonehenge and other sites will be discussed further in the Galactic Dragon chapter coming up shortly.

Recently I began working with a small group of ladies from across the globe with the intention of working energetically with sites and the dragons that care for them. Below is my experience from one of these evenings.

I initially connected with the Dragon of the Tor of Glastonbury. She was joined by a fire and water dragon (I have infrequently worked with elemental dragons) to clear the surface and emotional rubbish left behind by us as humans and to support her. This took some time.

From there we (Tor Dragon and I) linked into the dragon song line at the Tor. Tor Dragon took me along song lines to Avebury, starting at the Sun Circle, through the Moon Cove, through the Tolkien trees and then up the Avenue to the Sanctuary, Silbury Hill and the West Kennet Long Barrow. All felt clear and flowing as it should do. There are some who work hard at Avebury to keep the land and energies clear.

From Avebury we went to Stonehenge where we were met by a wall of black gloop – this is the only way I can describe it. There I saw two dragons chained, one on each side of the Henge. I was joined by Fire and Water Dragons once more and two Galactic Dragons. The Galactic Dragons gave me a sword of white light to release the first dragon and a blue sword of light to free the second.

I invited Tatiana in (she is a dragon who works with one of the other ladies in our group) to take them for healing. She informed me the dragons wished to stay at Stonehenge but she would check in on them. They felt weak and energetically they were a shadow of their true brightness and magnificence. There is further work to do.

Before we left, the Galactic Dragons showed me how they can clear vast areas with what felt like sound waves. Imagine dropping a pebble into a glass-smooth pool of water and seeing how the disturbed water ripples out in ever increasing circles. This is what they did from the centre of Stonehenge. As the ripples faded, they repeated the process and kept repeating it until the ripples gently kept flowing outwards, clearing and clarifying the energy of the land for miles.

Communing with the Land

The dragons and our land need our help to keep the energy that flows through it clear. This work can be carried out remotely but in truth there is nothing better than to sit and commune with the land (and connect to dragon within it). It nourishes our soul and supports our very existence.

Dragons are not only found within sacred sites, of course. They can be found within mountain ranges, caves, large bodies of water such as lakes and lochs and anywhere there is a large outdoor space.

Meditation with the Dragons of the Land

This meditation can be carried out either remotely or in person at a place of your choosing.

1. Take a few moments to centre yourself and connect with your heart.
2. Spend a little time walking around your chosen place, feeling into finding the perfect spot to sit (or stand).
3. Once settled, take a few deep breaths and observe the view, watching the sun, shadows and clouds dance. Watch and listen to the voice of the place. Allow yourself some time to adjust to its vibration and frequency. Allow yourself to ground deeply, anchoring your energy deep into the heart of Mother Earth.
4. Invite the Dragon of the Land to join with you. Feel their presence as your energy connects.

- ➤ What do you sense from them?
- ➤ What colour are they?
- ➤ How can you help?
- ➤ How can you be of service to the land and the dragons?
- ➤ What action are they asking you to take?
- ➤ What is their message for you?

You can stay here and work with the dragon for as long as you feel guided.

Connecting with the Dragons of the Land

You can connect with the Dragons of the Land in a variety of ways. You do not always need to be in meditation to connect with them although they do tell me this is the best way.

To connect with them, kick off your shoes and walk barefoot with quiet contemplation, taking your focus inwards and to the Earth. Quieten your mind using the mindful breathing exercise if this helps. Feel the earth, soil, sand or rock beneath your feet. Feel for that connection to the Earth, the land and the dragon within it. What do you sense, know, see, feel and hear?

Sit down and take out your notepad and begin to write or sketch. Do so without thought or judgement. Simply be with yourself, the land and the dragons. Sitting with and in the stillness is a powerful tool to use.

You may find it helpful to use your five senses if you find your mind is jumping about or you feel unsettled in any way. You may like to ask yourself some questions to start you off.

- What can I see? Describe the landscape, sky, clouds, people ...
- What can I feel? The ground beneath you, the air, the sun ...
- What can I smell? The air, wood smoke, cigarettes, the earth, what else?
- What can I hear? The birds, the wind, people talking, music, drumming, traffic ...
- What can I taste? Are you near water, the sea? Can you taste the salt in the air? Are drinking coffee or chewing gum?

When you are ready, begin to feel into the landscape.

- Imagine who has been here before you.
- What was it like here; how has it changed over the years?
- What impressions are you receiving? How are you receiving them? Can you see, them, sense or know them?
- Are there dragons within the land?
- What do they feel like?
- What colours, shape and size are they?
- Are they sleeping?
- Do they have a specific role within the land here?

Jot down anything and everything that floats through your mind and consciousness. Do not think about it or analyse it – just simply do it. Do not sit and reread what you have just written or critique what you have drawn. Stay with the energy of the moment, moment to moment, minute to minute.

Feel for the messages of the land. Seek out and ask the Dragon of the Land, the guardian of the site, to join you. Ask them how you can help. What do they need from you? Note it all down; do not judge, think or question.

Stay in this space for as long as feels right. When you are ready, pick up all your things including any emotional baggage and take them with you, thanking the land and the dragons when you leave.

Once you have gone through this exercise, your mind, body and soul should have connected to the Earth beneath you. You hopefully feel grounded and quieter within yourself. Once you have come back to you, your energies should be feeling less scattered.

Do not reread or look at what took place for at least 24 to 48 hours. Allow yourself to process it all in your own time. When you take a look at what you wrote, I think you will be pleasantly surprised at the insights, wisdom and understanding that came through.

I have filled around 20 journals over the years with all kinds of ramblings, everything from worrying about the family to talking with the dragons, meditations and dragon Q&As (this was their preferred way of communicating with me for a long time). But I never reread any of it until I need it.

While creating and writing this book I have spent many days going back through the journals, marking up what was possibly useful. I have found some truly mindblowing information dating back to the early and mid 2000s. Our dragons truly are our best teachers!

Dragons and Sound

All the dragons enjoy and can be connected with via sound. The Dragons of the Land carry the frequency of the drum and the didgeridoo. I feel that both of these instruments carry the heartbeat and frequency of Mother Earth.

You may like to gather together a group of friends at a particular site to connect with the Earth and drum and chant to connect with the dragon there. You will find what works for you and the lands surrounding you. Follow your own inner guidance.

Approach this in much the same way as you did with the previous exercise. You may like to start with a short grounding meditation to connect with the Earth and set a group intention for healing. This can be on a personal level, planetary level, global level and so on. It does not matter what you choose to do as long as you approach it with a grounded open heart and intention. You may like to tune into the land and the dragon and ask what they need. Once you are ready as group, you can begin.

1. As your focus shifts and you connect to the sound and the land, have an awareness of how the land around you responds. Feel for messages, feelings and sensations. Listen to your inner knowing, feel for the dragon and invite them to join you. This will aid your dragon connection and support the work in clearing, healing and repairing the dragon song lines, which I talk about in more detail in chapter 14.
2. Remember the dragons are always respectful so bear this in mind when working with sound, particularly in an outdoor space and even more so if there are other people also working nearby.

Chanting with the Dragons

Another sound that dragons resonate with is the human voice. All the dragons like chanting. You can explore this to find which ones you connect with. If they resonate with you, they certainly will with your dragons. Chanting can also be added to any other sound work you wish to do. Think about what suits your and the dragons' intentions and your surroundings.

Below are a couple of example chants that I have worked with over the years with the dragons. Try them out and see how you get on. Over time you will find your own chants. If, unlike me, you are musical, you can create your own to suit the rhythm of the work you are doing. Experiment and experience it all. None of these things are ever wasted.

Chant One – Earth is my Body

Earth my body
Water my blood
Air my breath
Fire my spirit

Repeat as many times as you feel you need to.

Chant Two – Mother I Feel You

Mother I feel you under my feet,
Mother I hear your heartbeat
Mother I feel you under my feet,
Mother I hear your heartbeat

heya heya heya yah heya heya ho
heya heya heya heya heya ho

Mother I hear you in the River song,
eternal waters flowing on and on
Mother I hear you in the River song,
eternal waters flowing on and on

heya heya heya yah heya heya ho
heya heya heya heya heya ho

Father I see you when the Eagle flies,
Light of the Spirit going to take us higher

Father I see you when the Eagle flies,
Light of the Spirit going to take us higher

heya heya heya yah heya heya ho
heya heya heya heya heya ho

Mother I feel you under my feet,
Mother I hear your heartbeat
Mother I feel you under my feet,
Mother I hear your heartbeat

I found the lyrics to this on lyrics-on.net

In short, all the Dragons of the Land resonate with sounds that relate to Mother Earth, and the Galactic Dragons are drawn in by (and resonate to) higher frequencies.

DRAGON TIP

DRAGONS OFTEN COMMUNICATE WITH US THROUGH OUR INNER KNOWING – LEARN TO USE AND TRUST IT.

CHAPTER

9

Moon Phases and Dragons

Working with the dragons and the moon can add an extra dimension and a touch of magic and power to your life and dragon work. The moon carries immense power. She affects the tides of the oceans with the pull of gravity that in turn has a smaller impact on our weather. Working with your energy, unconscious and conscious mind and inner compass with the moon combined with the dragons can be life changing and liberating.

Within the realms of my work with the dragons I only work with the new and full moon energy although there are other phases within the moon's cycle as it waxes and wanes between the full and new moons. The moon shimmers and floats her way through her various phases over approximately a 28-day period. She begins life as the dark moon. This is to do with the way the Earth, moon and sun line up, when our visual of the moon is hidden from us (turning her invisible).

Her journey across our skies goes like this:

⫸ New/dark moon
⫸ Waxing moon
⫸ Full moon
⫸ Waning moon

When the moon is leaving her dark phase we begin to see slivers of her reappearing as she builds toward the full moon. This is known as the waxing moon. Once she has reached her zenith of fullness, she begins the journey back toward the new moon. This is called the waning moon.

The moon herself has played her part over a millennia, with our ancestors plotting when to plant, move location, hunt and gather, and I am sure so much more. In her fullness she shows us a guiding light as darkness falls. In her darkness she urges us to gather our self and our energies together.

The moon is a powerful ally to work with and understanding how her transit across the sky affects you is incredibly liberating. Gaining a better understanding of the moon's phases, how they impact your life and how you react to them (and in turn following your inner flow) can offer great insights.

I began following the moon phases about 20 years ago due to the effect it was having upon my husband. He used to be very affected by the full moon. His responses and reactions around this, although totally unconscious, impacted massively upon family life and the equilibrium at home.

Working with the New Moon

Both the full and new moons have a completely different effect on our life, mental attitude and emotion balance. So I will begin this section with a little bit of information about the new moon and its properties.

We are made of around 60 per cent water, and water represents our emotions. The new moon connects with our subconscious and offers us an opportunity to reflect on where and who we are and what we wish to see or manifest for ourselves (and the world if we are working on a larger scale). In effect, the new moon is saying to you, "What do you require? What do you wish to take forward and birth into the world with the waxing to the full moon using the moon energies?"

Using the moon and in this case specifically the new moon energies, the dragons encourage you to go within to explore what works for you and what you wish for. What would you like to manifest into the world for yourself? What do you wish to create for yourself? Many people term this "new moon wishes", which I will talk about in more detail further into this chapter.

Working with new moon energies offers so much potential for growth and personal understanding, for it guides you in creating a deeper connection and understanding of yourself – knowing and exploring your own inner uniqueness, quirks and strengths and where you can build and explore. The new moon is therefore for inner work. It is a time of reflecting, tuning into your body and where your energy is flowing.

In effect what you are doing here is planting your seeds in this quiet dark phase of the moon. This is also a perfect time to choose where you wish to see your life grow and change under the tutelage and guidance of your personal dragons and of course the Galactic Dragons. All you need to do is ask them to join you.

Tapping into your inner guidance and knowing at this time is perfect for manifesting and also for laying the foundations for your life's bigger plans. The dragons remind you that you are the master creator of your world, sitting with the new moon and feeling and contemplating what you want rather than what you do not want.

There are many moon phases. If you want to know more about these, you need to seek out Yasmin Boland's book *Moonology*. My dragons guided me to this book a few years ago when I was looking for something specific around working with the new moon energies.

Each new moon, like that of the sabbats which I talk about more in the following chapter, is a point in time to pause, re-evaluate and see where you are at energetically, emotionally, spiritually and of course physically. Sometimes you will not feel like setting plans and seeds in motion, especially during the colder winter months with the dark and cold weather.

When it is dark, cold and dreary outside, many of us do not feel like doing much at all, and that is fine.

The key to working this way is to recognize where your energy is and on an emotional, physical, mental and spiritual level to acknowledge where you are energetically. If you want to hibernate until spring, do so but do it consciously.

Some years ago I recognized I slowed down from October onwards. I was working with Bear energy at the time, and he was a huge part of my life for a few years. I retreated from the world. I continued to work and develop but at a slower pace, gaining perspective and deeper understanding of myself and my spiritual path along the way. As the sun returned, gaining height and potency in the sky, my energy shifted and I emerged any time from Imbolc to the Spring Equinox (see chapter 10).

If you wish to retreat from the world over the winter months until spring returns, so be it. But this does not mean you ignore life or the world (although it would be so nice to do so at times), but you can work with and delve into what and how you are feeling. Dive into it with your dragons and explore it. You do not have or need to do anything except recognize it and that in itself loosens everything up.

Sleep

By the time the moon is reaching for her new moon phase, our sleep has usually returned to a more normal pattern. Now we have the energy to think about and begin to nurture what we would like to see in our lives.

Although working with the energy of the new moon is often called new moon wishing, it goes deeper than that. Manifesting is all about alignment, feeling it; there is no attachment to its outcome of any kind. There is a sort of knowing that has no negative, doubt or fearful attachments around it. Remember that where attention goes, energy flows.

Here I will talk about all the possibilities that you wish to achieve and see more of in your life. But first, let us look at our need for "self-clutter". The dragons do not follow nor understand our need for self-clutter – things that clutter our lives and act as a distraction at best and a sticking plaster at worst. They are very much of the view that these things clutter our clarity especially if we are overfocused on them. That is not to say that you have to live a frugal life in solitude; as ever with the dragons it is all about finding a balance.

When it comes to working with new moon manifestation or moon wishing, you may have a wish for the right people (your tribe), a new job, more money or home life in alignment and balance with you and your energy. It may be that what you need is time or more love, understanding and patience, or it could be hope and clarity. There are no real rights or wrongs. You are highly unlikely to get the lottery numbers though.

On that note, a friend of mine was learning to use the pendulum for dowsing years ago so she thought for practise she would dowse for the lottery numbers. The winning number that came out that weekend was always the one next to the numbers she chose, but more importantly her pendulum went missing. She knew exactly where she had put it but spirit had whisked it away. This acts as reminder to her and us all that this work is not a party game nor should it be taken out of context.

This juncture could be the perfect time to return to your journaling work. Using your journal is a great way to work through your wishes, aims, dreams and aspirations, anything that makes your heart sing at this precise moment. What is it that gives you that rush of excitement and lifts your heart? What brings that inner smile of happiness?

Write down what you would like to accomplish, have or be in your life. Work through and list it all. Once this is complete you can settle on the ones that are most important to you now. It is these things that are at the nub and heart of manifesting.

What you do here does not need to be complicated. Pick one or two things at the most to work with, following the flow of your energy. As the moon waxes toward her fullness and the month marches ever onwards, remember to adjust course and set your sails as you need to.

As the month progresses some things take a little longer than others to manifest. The seeds of an idea sown now may take a couple of months and at times a few years to come to full fruition. At other times it can take place quite comfortably within a few weeks. It is always all about timing.

Manifesting with the New Moon

You can use a few options when manifesting with the new moon.

For your new moon wishes you may like to create an altar. This does not need to be anything complicated or large – a small table will do. It may take you a couple of days to prepare for this exercise – not all day, but building and focusing your intention. You may like to go into the garden and pick flowers, or take a walk along the beach to collect pebbles and seashells, or out into woods to pick up fallen twigs and leaves, nuts and so on. Remember to respect nature and do not remove anything from living trees and plants without first asking for their permission to use their energy for your wishes.

Once you have gathered together what you require (this will be different each time), take a few minutes to centre yourself, take some deep breaths and connect to the Earth. You may like to spend a few minutes meditating to clear your head and feel into your new moon wishes. The head and heart meditation works well here too.

On your table/altar you can place a candle of your favourite colour or scent, crystals, incense, an image of the dragon you want to work with (this can be from my deck or any other image or deck that is right for the work you are doing) some flowers, leaves, twigs, etc, depending on the time of year. Follow what feels right and connects with your new moon intentions.

1. Write out your new moon wishes.
2. Lay all your items out, including your new moon wishes, on your table in a way that feels right. Many people use a circle for this purpose or have a mandala cloth or mat for this purpose. Metatron's cube or flower of life are good starting points if you would like some structure if you are new to setting up altar space and grids. Take your time and move things around if you need to.
3. When all is complete you can light your candle or incense. Spend some time in this quiet space aligning yourself with your intention. Feel it in your body to complete the task. Once you do, your new moon wish has taken place – it has materialized.
4. Enjoy the solitude and quiet contemplation of the space.

The above moon ritual can be used on its own or you can tie it in with the work below, working with Magic and Manifestation from my Oracle card deck.

Manifesting Visualization

You have so far whittled down and sorted out what you would like more of in your life. Here the dragons Magic and Manifestation from my Oracle deck invite you to sit with them and connect with them to help bring your hopes, dreams and specific moon wishes to fruition.

These two impressive dragons will ask you searching and probing questions. They will likely urge you to go deeper with your desire, questioning your alignment at this time. The dragons are good at prodding and poking, to make us feel into things more deeply to ensure that we are in full alignment with what we are asking for.

At times there may be blocks around your request. If so, Magic and Manifestation will guide you when these surface. These blocks can be anything from self-doubt, fears, guilt or worry to not being good enough, impostor syndrome and more. All of this comes up when we begin manifesting and wanting things for ourselves that we do not believe we have the right to or do not feel we are worthy of.

The key to successful manifestation is to feel it, rejoice in that feeling and become comfortable with those feelings. When blocks appear, this shows you where you are not quite in alignment with your dreams or that these are not in alignment with you. If there is any uncomfortableness, this shows where you possibly need to do further work that can be released and carried out at the time of the full moon.

This is the beauty of doing this work. It is ever the onion skin, gently peeling away the layers, even of old stuff that you thought was done and dusted. It can be so irritating and frustrating when the same old issue raises its ugly head again.

Welcome to the joys of being a human work in progress.

Working with Magic and Manifestation

Working with manifestation is not so much about visualizing; it is more about feeling and knowing. That comfortable almost solidness of "yeah this is good", of feeling so right and practical and in alignment. The beauty of this is that it guides you to work further and deeper, stretching you to grow. And of course you have your dragons beside you guiding your way.

Take a few minutes to centre and ground yourself. Then take a couple of long slow deep breaths in and invite Magic and Manifestation to join you.

Your request may go something like this:

1. "Magic and Manifestation, I ask for you to join me in bringing my new moon wishes to fullness."
2. Visualize them in front of you: the silvery purple of Magic holding his pentagram and bright gold of Manifestation with the shimmering Metatron's Cube behind him.
3. Once you are sitting comfortably, begin to feel what it would be like to achieve your new moon wishes. Visualize this so it takes shape. Does it have a colour texture? How does it feel to be in that space, that person, that situation?
4. Continue feeling into your wish, your dream. How does it feel? What does it smell like? Where are you? Allow the feeling of joy, of expansive euphoria, to flow through you. Allow it to build in you, to fill you.
5. Gather the energy in your heart chakra. Feel it build and fill there, totally and completely.
6. When you are ready, still holding the image of Magic and Manifestation in your mind, release the flow of your new moon wishes to these two impressive and

most magical of all the dragons. Feel it flow from you to them, releasing the knowing and the joy.

The dragons will take your new moon wishes up into the heavens, stratosphere and Universe. They will release it back to you at the perfect time. This is where magic takes place. Your task is now to follow the signs, synchronicities and the knowings being passed back to you, to take the steps laid out before you.

You sometimes need patience to do this and being patient is not a human strength. It is certainly not one of mine. So let it go, give it wings and give it to Magic and Manifestation. Allow them to do the heavy lifting of the how, the why and the when. They will return it to you at the perfect time.

Working with the new moon is all about planting seeds and nurturing ideas and plans. It is a point to pause and reflect and offers an opportunity for any personal or spiritual work and much deeper personal understanding.

Full Moon

Now we come to the full moon. The word lunacy comes from the full moon; we can all go a bit "bat shit crazy" around the time it appears. The full moon can pull the tides of entire oceans and to a lesser effect have an impact upon our weather systems so it is hardly surprising that it affects us so deeply.

The energy of the full moon can be so intense but the beauty of this is that it is a time of release and letting go. The trade off, as I have discovered, is that it also brings everything into our conscious minds. The stuff you have been ducking and diving and brushing under the carpet. The emotions you have been squishing down. All the avoidance tucked away on an unconscious or an emotional level comes at us with a full force 500 watt power at the full moon. This can be a painful, emotional and bumpy ride.

Sleep can be disrupted by both the full moon and the new moon. Dreams can be a little more intense at these times, sleep can become illusive and moods and emotions erratic, leading to frayed tempers. This is the power of the moon! So it can be beneficial to gain a better understanding of the moon faces and phases and how you are affected by them and follow her ebbing and flowing as she moves through waning to waxing.

If the new moon is for inner work and manifesting, the full moon is for outer work and the physical world. I think of the new moon as our private world of the unseen, as in our thoughts, emotions, dreams, hopes and aspirations. The full moon is our reality and a physical representation of what goes on outside us – our "doing" life, our work, home, etc. This brings everything into focus and is the illuminator if you know what to look for.

At the full moon we can often feel "wired and tired" as my herbalist calls it. As the moon waxes to her full beauty and glory, she can leave us feeling fairly fractious and unsettled, irritable and ungrounded, sometimes to the point of being spacey, tense and terse.

The full moon is about completion. She has moved through her dark moon phase sliver by sliver to come to complete fullness. As she moves through these phases, she has brought gifts and understanding: the dreaming, the action taken, the seeds planted and the wheels put into motion from the new moon, gaining roots and growth until everything reaches the perfect pause point once more.

Do you see the pattern? How our natural world and working with the phases of the moon along with the turning of the year urges us and affects us? These are moments of reflection; of creating time to stop, re-evaluate and reposition ourselves and our inner compass. The fullness of the moon offers you a chance to chart, plot and acknowledge your growth and achievements since the new moon.

With each of her faces and phases, the moon offers an opportunity twice each month to reset your sails. You can use this time to evaluate where your excitement and energy was at the new moon and to recognize where it may have cooled off at the time of the full moon. Your energy will flow through the air with the changing seasons and the moon's phases. Learn to recognize and flow with it.

I used to have two weeks, one week either side of the full moon, where I could barely function. At times sleep was so elusive, my mind jumping about all over the place, and inspiration proved to be thin on the ground, mainly due to a lack of sleep and being fuelled on caffeine. This in turn would take my intuition and inspiration with it.

Once I found and understood this I altered how I worked. Now nearer the new moon I carry out work that requires my focus and free flowing connection with the Universe and the dragons. This is when I am most productive and receptive. Around the full moon I take it easy where I can. I have to almost cut out caffeine and any kind of stimulants such as sugar, chocolate, etc. – basically anything I enjoy! I had to learn to stop giving myself a hard time for not working at full capacity. I had to give myself permission to take time off and out.

With all that understanding, the energy of the moon affects me less now as I began to work with it rather than against it. Now life flows a great deal easier.

The full moon is the perfect time for releasing, clearing and letting go. The letting go can be on any and every level, such as old habits, thought patterns or negative traps you may have fallen into. This is also the perfect time to make use of the energy of the full moon for forgiveness, releasing all that does not support you and your spiritual quest. So once more you may find yourself back again with fear, agitation, anger and guilt, any kind of emotional pain and belief that no longer holds a place at your table.

The full moon shines a light on what requires your attention on an inner level and of course what needs to be let go of in your physical world. This can be people, jobs, relationships, homes, etc. You can use the energy of the full moon to do those clearing out jobs that you have been putting off, such as clearing out your wardrobe. The clothes that no longer fit yet you keep kidding yourself you will get back into them. (Yes, I know that one well – my favourite pair of jeans is going to have to go at the next full moon!) Use the time to go through your pantry and kitchen cupboards, clean out your car (another "to do" job for me!).

This in the simplest of terms can bring clarity and order, particularly if you find yourself feeling a little overwhelmed by the moon's full intensity shining itself at full power on your life. If you are not ready to face it head on just yet do a little bit of decluttering. As you declutter and go through those emotions by ditching or donating, you begin to shed layers that you have been unconsciously hanging on to. This is incredibly powerful and liberating.

Emotions are high on the agenda when it comes to the full moon; everything is heightened. This means that everything and anything can float to the surface so the full moon is a time to be gentle with yourself. Be prepared to shed a tear as you let go, to feel emotional, anger even. This is OK. This is all good. The key to these surfacing emotions is to embrace them and acknowledge them. They are surfacing to show that you can do this and it is time to move on to the next phase of your incredible life.

If it takes a few days to do this then so be it. The dragons say, "Rome wasn't built in a day, but it would have been if they'd used dragons."

We often think and do "outside" of ourselves but the moon reminds us that she is often a mirror of our inner workings. So give yourself permission to forgive yourself in whichever way is needed right now, big or small. Your outer world is a free flowing reflection of your inner world; the dragons taught me this many moons ago.

Here the dragons invite you to return once more to your journal. You can use your journal to review what you need to let go of from your "clutter bank". This could be to do with emotions, thoughts and ways of being. You can carry out visualization and release it all to the dragons, using the meditation of the blue silk cloth we talked of earlier in chapter eight or pass it to Magic and Manifestation. You can also use the other meditations at this time for anything that does not serve you and is holding you back.

Any kind of doubts and upsets can all be released within the energy of the full moon because as she begins to wane her way back to the new moon she takes with her everything you do not need. She has done her job and you now know what you can let go. This is the beauty of working with all the moon phases. Everything is in transition, in movement and never stationary – and you do not need to be either.

We are constantly evolving souls. We openly flow with the tides, the moon and our energy. Here with the dragons to guide you, know and accept that we are all a work in progress. Give yourself a bit of a break and allow things to just "be" – you will thank yourself for it.

DRAGON TIP

WHERE INTENTION GOES, ENERGY FLOWS.

CHAPTER

10

Dragons and Walking the Wheel of the Year

EIGHT FESTIVALS AND FOUR DIRECTIONS

Some dragons follow the energy of the wheel of the year. This particular journey for me began with Fire Dragon around Mabon (the autumn equinox) a few years ago.

I had received a message asking if I would take the dragons and work with a group of people at a small camp. I was buttering my toast, trying to formulate a polite refusal, when Fire Dragon literally swept in through the kitchen window almost knocking me off my feet with her power and energy.

I was told I would attend and that "we" would hold a dragon fire ceremony based around the late summer festival of Mabon. The whole ceremony was given to me in seconds, even down to the start and finish times. Fire Dragon was bang on the money with the timings and the ceremony. I have lost count of how many times I have held that ceremony with Fire Dragon over the years.

Like much of the dragon work and in particular with the Dragons of the Land, the energy of a dragon ceremony connects with our moon phases. For this reason I try to hold these as close as possible to either the full or new moon and ideally with one of the festivals from the Celtic year. The dragons tend to let me know when they wish the next one to be held.

Within my deck is Herne (an aspect of the divine masculine) who connects to the Winter Solstice, also known as Yule, and divine feminine who connects to the Summer Solstice or the mid-summer festival. Divine feminine came to me around the time of the Summer Solstice way back, and for a long time that is what she was known as until she announced that she is an aspect of the divine feminine! These two make up one of the Guardian pairs in the deck.

The dragons love the wheel of the year and had been nagging at me for some time to begin to walk it. I kept my eye out for the right teacher to learn from, to do this work and learning within a group setting, to deepen my understanding from either a shamanic or pagan point of view. But as is the dragons' way with me that was not be my path. I was to walk it alone and learn and discern from it under their guidance alone.

I have followed the flow of the seasons and the major festivals for about 15 years. Around five years ago I began following the festivals and the turning of year more closely, learning about them and the ebb and flow of the energy of the land and the seasons. In 2020 I began to walk the wheel of the year with intention as guided by my dragons.

One Samhain I attended a goddess workshop in Avebury working with the Goddess Ceridwin. That afternoon I also planned to walk the labyrinth as the start of my walking the wheel of the year with my dragons. The dragons had told me that I was to walk it at sunset at Samhain. By the time I had driven across two counties from Avebury to Winchester, climbed the hill and walked the labyrinth the sun was just setting. I did not set out with that in mind as such; it is the way the day panned out. As ever the dragons are right!

Following the Celtic Year

The Celtic new year begins at Samhain (Halloween – although there are varying opinions on this) on 31 October. Each of the other festivals follow around every six weeks. The timings are these on or around the following dates.

- ⫸ Samhain – 31 October
- ⫸ Yule – 21 December

◈ Imbolc – 1 February
◈ Spring Equinox – 21 March
◈ Beltane – 1 May
◈ Summer Solstice – 21 Jun
◈ Lammas – 1 August
◈ Autumn Equinox – 21 September

If like me you wish to begin a journey of deepening discovery of the self, honouring the Earth and the everturning of the wheel under your dragons' guidance you can. You do not need to wait until Samhain. Your journey can begin whenever you feel guided that this is the right time for you. You do not need to walk the labyrinth to do this; this was simply what I was guided to do by my dragons.

You may like to begin your journey at one of the festivals below, although it is not important that you do so. To walk the wheel with your dragons all you need is intent and an open heart and mind and to be receptive for whatever emerges and transpires for you.

You can mark it simply with the lighting of a candle and setting an intention for the particular festival you are honouring. Or you may like to gather with friends, to create a more formal event, share stories, hopes and dreams with the energy of the sabbats or festival at the time. You can light candles, be creative and arty, using natural materials to make wreaths, art, corn dollies and more. You can use and create space for reflection and meditation. There are no limits or right ways to do this. You can ask your dragons for guidance and follow their messages.

Each of the four main festivals over the course of the year has its own element and direction. These are:

◈ Winter Solstice: 21 December – the element is Earth
◈ Summer Solstice: 21 June – the element is Fire
◈ Spring Equinox: 21 March – the element is Air
◈ Autumn Equinox: 21 September – the element is Water

These festivals roughly take place around the 21st of the month, although they do move around from year to year.

The other festivals (the cross quarters) are known as the four great fire festivals (perfect for dragon work!). If you want to know more about working with the seasons and wheel of the year, there are some brilliant books on this by Glennie Kindred.

These festivals are:

- Imbloc: 1 February – the element is Air
- Beltane: 1 May – the element is Earth
- Lammas: 1 August – the element is Fire
- Samhain: 31 October – the element is Water

Elemental Dragons

It makes sense that the Elemental Dragons connect to the elements. These Dragons of the Land have four directions with their associated element of Earth, Air, Fire and Water and connect with the wheel of the year. All of them can be called upon to help, guide and gain deeper understanding of any situation at any point but their most active and potent time is around the festival they relate to. I have worked extensively with Fire Dragon in ceremony over the last few years and she is incredibly powerful. She will often show herself from October onwards although I have worked with her during the Summer Solstice, Mabon and Yule.

I will discuss all of the dragons in the way they have given the details to me including their direction and their elements. Remember here that you are working with dragons so if you call upon them you will get what you need but you may not like it!

Air Dragon – Spring Equinox – East

The sun is slowly warming the Earth once more, and we are seeing life return from the dark soil. We are reminded as always through the wheel of the year of life, death and rebirth. Here at Spring Equinox we bear witness to life.

Air Dragon gives us breath so we can breathe and wings so we can fly. Air is also a representation of our minds, mental attitude and acts as timely reminder that we can fly high if we so chose. Air Dragon acts as a great reminder that you are not your mind or your thoughts, and also connects you to your spiritual side. Air Dragon and Spring Equinox are the perfect partners for setting intentions and giving your dreams wings.

Fire Dragon – Summer Solstice – South

The sun has reached its peak within the wheel of the year. We still have the lazy, warm filled days ahead of us and the bounty of the Earth yet to harvest. We also recognize the days will gradually shorten as the sun moves across our skies.

Fire Dragon is a game changer. She is mighty and powerful and her time is the Summer Solstice and the height of summer. She reveals to us our fullness of power, our strengths and all that we can celebrate. She encourages us to be outwardly expressive, to explore and celebrate all we have in life, to review our purpose and to reach for our goals.

Water Dragon – Autumn Equinox – West

With the continuing turning of the wheel of the year, the sun is slowly losing her power. We celebrate the fullness of the year with harvests of fruits and corn. This is a time of great abundance, with warm days and cooler nights.

Water Dragon is the time of the Autumn Equinox. Here you can call upon her guidance if you wish to do any kind of emotional and creative work as she will undoubtedly add power to your spiritual work. Here she encourages and supports your personal healing as you mature and grow with each passing year. Working with her can be somewhat emotional and liberating. This is the perfect time to review the previous few months and acknowledge how far you have come.

Earth Dragon – Winter Solstice – North

With the arrival of Yule we embrace the longest night (shortest day). Yule is truly a time of inner reflection, spiritual insight and wisdom gained from the preceding months. Everything begins life in darkness to be given time to germinate and take root to emerge with the returning of the sun as the wheel of the year turns once more.

Here you sow your seeds, ideas and thoughts for the coming year. You may like to call upon Earth Dragon to ground your dreams and nurture your seeds over the coming months.

Creating Ceremony with the Dragons

Below is the fire ceremony that I use with Fire Dragon. I use this at various points throughout the year. You can adapt it to incorporate the various elements of Earth, Air, Fire and Water to fit your intentions and what you wish to create or clear. You can take guidance from any of the elemental dragons on the best way to do this and also follow your own inner guidance and intuition.

The ceremony on the following pages is set with the energy and intention of Yule but it can be adapted to incorporate any of the festivals above.

Yule Intentions

Yule is probably my favourite of all the festivals within the wheel of the year. Here at midwinter (I am actually writing this on Yule morning) we have the celebration of Yule. We welcome the gradual return of the sun, the promise of the days very slowly beginning to lengthen as light returns once more to our world.

Often at Yule I will hold a dragon fire ceremony as it is the perfect point in the year to pause and reflect, although Yule is actually the element of Earth. These are my thoughts about Yule. When you begin to walk the wheel of the year with your dragons you will find your own thoughts and observations about each one as you move through the seasons.

Yule, the longest night, heralds the returning of the sun as we finally welcome back the light. This particular solstice is the time to reflect inwards, where it can feel like time stands still for a while. Use this to anchor that which you wish to bring forth with the returning sun.

The end of the year is the time to reflect over the last few months to see just how far you have come, to celebrate your successes and achievements and to acknowledge whatever may need work, healing or releasing on an inner personal level. But mostly this is the time to be thankful for the life you have with those who share it with you and have been walking the path with you.

This solstice offers you a chance to have some quiet time for yourself away from the hubbub of everyday life, work pressures and all that it entails. We have three days where the light/sun stands still in the sky, from 20 to 23 December. We can take our cue from this and do the same.

With this reflection and the returning of the sun new life begins to form. The late winter flowers such as snowdrops will eventually poke their heads through the cold dark soil. Bulbs planted the autumn before begin their slow growth toward the light. We too can share in this retuning of the sun.

We can anchor our dreams, hopes and aspirations. We have time over the darker days to consider what we would like to take into the turning of the year – how we would like our year to be different or improved upon from the last. With the everturning of the wheel and seasons, we are being offered a chance to once more be reborn, to take our first steps into the new year, the new cycle of life, with the slowly returning warmth of the sun, giving us the strength and power to do so.

Over the darker evenings from Mabon (Autumn Equinox) to Yule we have been rooting ideas, plans, thoughts and more. From Yule to the Imbolc or maybe as far as the Spring Equinox we have the opportunity to work with our conscious mind – to set our intentions, our conscious hopes and dreams.

What are your intentions for you for the coming months (from Yule to Imbolc)? These are very different from setting a New Year's resolution. There is no guilt or pressure tied into these intentions. These are set in motion to guide you so you follow your own personal energy flow and feelings. Follow the flow that the dragons have been guiding you along since you began this journey.

Reflection Point

Take a few minutes to think about and feel what your energy is telling you. What intentions suit you and your purpose now? How do they feel? Do they feel empowering and exciting?

If they do not, they are not in alignment with your energy at this time. So it is best not to follow them any further at the moment – they can wait. There will be more important ones for you to explore that are in alignment with your energy and what you and your soul and divine purpose need at this time.

As you walk this path you can adjust your course as you need to. Nothing here is set in stone. You can use the festival of Imbolc to re-evaluate where you are. This is the beauty of walking the wheel of the year, especially with the dragons. They will nudge and guide you if you are prepared to listen.

Preparing for a Ceremony with Fire Dragon

This Fire Dragon ceremony can be used at any time throughout the year. The example given below is the one I use at Yule but you can adapt it to suit the time of year and your needs. It is always best carried out outdoors and with a group so do prepare in advance and dress for the conditions. There is nothing worse than being cold while you are meditating! You will also require a fire pit or a cauldron (something to hold fire safely), pens, paper and candles.

Before you begin the ceremony below take a few minutes in quiet contemplation to consider what you have achieved over the year. Give thanks for those achievements and successes, to those who have walked beside you, both in the physical and spiritual. Also think about what you wish to continue to nurture over the coming months into the spring.

Allow your thoughts and ideas to germinate while you absorb the landscape and the stillness of the world around you. Feel into it; sense the power of the natural world.

Accept the trials and tribulations of the year. Try not to fall in judgement here, to tie yourself in knots with them. Accept them for what they were or are, and adjust your course today whether emotionally, mentally, physically or spiritually as you need to.

Bear in mind that the ideas and thoughts you came into the ceremony with may well be very different by the time you have completed it. A change of course may be necessary so allow that natural flow to take place. What you think you want to release and embrace may also shift. Simply allow it to do so. Offer no judgement or reasoning; let it flow over you and see what materializes for you.

The ceremony below is best carried out in a group so it is written in this way. You can of course adapt it for working on your own.

Yule Dragon Fire Ceremony

Settle in quiet contemplation, focusing on your breath and inwards to a place of centre and balance. This is a space in which you peruse and consider, going to that deep inner wisdom. Ultimately the plan is quell your tumbling thoughts, keeping your mind quiet and body relaxed. The head and heart meditation (chapter one) is good to use here.

For the next sections, take as long as you need but do not overthink. Go with your first thoughts, feelings and impressions for both lists. Everyone taking part needs a sheet of paper, ideally A4 size folded in half lengthways.

At the top of the first column write a heading of Aims, Wishes, Ambitions, Desires or similar. Beneath this heading list all the things you would like to nurture over the winter months. The seeds you are planting in readiness for next spring. Things you would like to work on, get grounded, start and learn. Anything and everything you would like to do or try to do. Write in the column whatever grabs your attention. You can even draw pictures if this helps.

At the top of the other column write a heading of Release, Rubbish, Let Go or even Crap, whatever you decide. In this column list all the stuff you no longer want or need in your life. The stuff that holds you back – old habits, friendships or relationships, jobs – all the garbage you feel is negative and detrimental to your life going forward. All those things that hold no place at your table now.

Once both lists are complete, fold your paper in half so your list can't be seen. Then it is time to meet your fire dragon.

1. Visualize yourself on an early evening walk somewhere out in nature in a rural setting with woodland, paths and fields. The stars are just beginning to blink into life in the darkening sky. You can smell wood smoke and the faint aroma of damp earth. There is a little nip to the early evening breeze.

2. As you make your way along the path an owl swoops down in front of you. You feel drawn to follow it as it glides silently along leading you forward to a large clearing and he settles in a nearby tree to observe the events. There is a large log with a seat cut into it, just the right size for you. Someone has kindly left you a beautifully made woollen blanket to put over your knees, protecting you against the evening chill. There is a small fire set inside a circle of stones. You spend a few minutes watching the flames dance as timber crackles and pops. Off to one side a pile of wood has been left for your fire. You add a couple of logs and retake your seat, watching the flames dance and flicker.

3. As you watch the fire begins to take form and from it raises Fire Dragon. She is mighty and powerful, the colour of the flames in reds, oranges and yellows with the smallest hint of blues and purples. The fire continues to burn brightly within the ring of stones. For all her might and power you know you are completely safe with Fire Dragon. You regard each other, looking deeply into one another's eyes. You can see the fire reflected and burning brightly in hers as she looks back at you.

4. She asks of you, "What is it that you wish to change? What in your life is to be transmuted or erased?" She warns, "Once spoken, the words can't be revoked; that is the power of Fire Dragon." The dragons all urge us to fly from our gilded cages. Once the words are spoken they can't be undone. Consider anything that no longer serves you, that you can release to Fire Dragon

to be transmuted, clearing your path and way forward or releasing you from the past. Ponder this thought before giving it life. Be sure in your heart. What you release to her can be from the list you made earlier or something else entirely. Are you ready to let it go?

5. When you are ready let the thoughts, feelings and attachments flow from you to Fire Dragon. Watch her sparkle and crackle as everything you let go of is released and transmuted by her. Allow as much time as you need here. Take a few moments to see how you feel, all the time being aware of Fire Dragon in your presence. Allow your energies to settle into a new rhythm.

6. Now we are going to take the second part of your list: your wishes, dreams, hopes and aims that you want to nurture over the coming months. Release that list and anything else to Fire Dragon. This time her energy shimmers as she absorbs your dreams and choices, giving them energy and fire to aid their journey to fruition.

7. Fire Dragon takes a long and considered look at you, checking that you have finished and there is nothing else to add. She turns and walks around the fire, taking in one full circle as if this is the turning of the year. She stops directly in front of you, looking deeply into your eyes, questioning you. Are you sure you want this? For she is about to return your dreams, hopes and aspirations with her fire blessing, her energy to guide you in giving these life. If you accept, give her one clear nod of your head and she will release the energy back to you. You feel it warm your entire being. Let this settle in your energy; absorb it and sit with it.

8. Take your gaze back to the fire and the flames. The fire is getting low. As you watch the dying embers, Fire Dragon steps back into the circle of stones. With a flash of orange and red she is gone. The fire is slowly dwindling. You sit and watch and feel.

9. As you become aware of the chill in the air once more you know it is time to make your way back. You stand up, feeling lighter, happier and more settled maybe. You fold the blanket and put it on the seat. The fire is almost gone, just ash left now. Owl takes his place flying low in front of you, guiding you back along the path you trod earlier. The full moon is now high in the sky, giving everything a silvery glow and illuminating your way while the owl flies silently ahead.

10. Once you are back in open space, the owl takes his leave. You become aware of the sounds around you once you are back in the physical world but also a quiet stillness. Take this moment to light your tea lights or candles, holding the energy of the meditation.

Staying with the quiet stillness, take your place standing around the fire. One at a time step forward and place your negative list into the fire. If you want to take one last look at it then do so before placing it in the flames. Wait for the paper to be fully burned to ash before the next person takes their turn.

Once everyone has finished releasing their negative list to the fire, you can choose to hand over to the Fire Dragon your hopes and dreams, or you can hold onto them and take them home with you. It is completely up to you.

Energy of the Seasons

As with the moon phases, each festival invites you to pause and to reflect, not only to honour our beautiful planet and Gaia as a living breathing entity but to also honour yourself. As you work and walk through the everchanging face of the moon and the turning of the seasons, you will grow and develop from your intentions. Take a breath, a moment in time to truly reflect upon how far you have come. I think you will be pleasantly surprised.

My husband and I did this recently. We actually took some time to reflect on how far we have come, grown and changed in the last ten years and it was quite a shock. We are very different people now to who we were ten years ago. So I invite you to do this more frequently as you will not see the smaller steps you have taken yet these are often the most important ones.

DRAGON TIP

➤ *FEEL FOR THE DRAGONS WITHIN THE LANDS AROUND YOU.*

➤ *CONNECT MORE DEEPLY WITH THEM THOUGH SOUND.*

CHAPTER

11

Mary Magdalene and the Sapphire Ray Dragons

Within this chapter you will meet Magdalene and her Sapphire Ray Dragons. Mary Magdalene's presence at this time is bringing in a whole lot of new dragon energy. This energy is built around sovereignty (spiritual and personal) with the Sapphire Ray Dragons. This led me to think about sovereignty on a deeper level. What does it actually mean to us as individuals and more importantly how does it affect us? How can we apply it to our daily lives, and how does it impact upon our spirituality?

I would like you spend a few minutes thinking about sovereignty in the broader terms and on a spiritual and personal level. What does it mean to you? You might like to jot down the words and feelings that come to mind in your dragon journal. Here are some of mine:

➤ Courage
➤ Wisdom
➤ Power
➤ Wealth
➤ Empowerment

➤ Service
➤ Control
➤ Alignment
➤ Care
➤ Strength

Magdalene and Sovereignty

Magdalene poses quite a formidable presence when she shows up and shows us sovereignty in action. She carries the energy of quiet authority; she knows who she is and her place in the world. She is comfortable in her own presence and knows fully what that presence holds and means for her.

Her overarching energy is one of compassion and kindness. She said to me: "Do not mistake my kindness for weakness."

She shows you here beautifully that you can be strong yet kind, powerful yet gentle. You can set firm boundaries without compromising yourself or your energy.

DRAGON TALK

Magdelene is undoubtedly all about female power and women stepping into that birthright.

She says: "You are safe to discover who you are; you are not the hats or labels you wear, nor are you what others wish or say you are. You are not too big, too small, too shy, too brash, too loud, nor too quiet. Be brave, be beautiful, be you."

When I met her with the Sapphire Dragons she was striding purposefully toward me, with her hair blowing out behind her, flanked by two striking blue dragons. She looked and felt like a woman on a mission. The words "warrior queen" came to mind. She is very aware that our world is far from love and light. She also knows that as women we are stronger than we think, more intuitive than we believe and have more to offer than being labels to other people, whether this is as a mum, daughter, sister, wife, aunt, colleague, mentor or coach.

She adds here: "You are far more if only you would allow it – you can be sovereignty in action."

Magdalene and her dragons are represented with the colour blue – this can be anything from deep royal blue to the much paler hues. They carry the blueprint of empowerment and tradition – knowing where it has its place and when it needs to be left behind. Just because something has always been a certain way does not mean this has to continue for the sake of tradition. The world is constantly evolving and you too have the option and choice to move, evolve and grow with it.

Of course you can stay where you are, feeling stuck, disempowered and tossed about by the winds of change and lament how hard, difficult and unfair the world is because you do not like it. Or you can decide to change and grow. The dragons are fond of saying, "Be the change you wish to see."

We as a human collective have so much potential now, more than we have ever been offered in recent history, and we need to make choices to decide what serves us and what we need to ditch from our society, lives and consciousness.

Magdalene truly is a powerhouse so it is hardly surprising that she has seven dragons at her side. During the lead up to Lions' Gate in July 2021, Mary Magdalene reappeared (she initially made herself known when I was working on creating my dragon cards) and this time she brought with her the seven Sapphire Ray Dragons. The Sapphire Ray allows each of us to step up.

DRAGON TALK

Magdalene said to me: *"Reclaim your power, women and men; it is your birthright."*

She carried on, *"Women as individuals and collectively, we are ever-evolving souls; we must stand together and bring our collective wisdom to the table.*

"As a collective for centuries women have been silenced, crushed, disempowered, lived in servitude and pain, frequently at the hand of men. It is time to redress this, without malice, imbalance or passing sentence. Rise above it; know your value and worth not only as a woman, but as a priestess of dragon power and as a child of Earth.

"Now is the time of forgiveness and healing. For what is done can't be undone, you already know this, but the chains of the past no longer need to bind you."

Standing by My Sisters

I love how the dragons and the Universe work hand in claw. Around the time I was preparing this chapter and working with Magdalene, I discovered the book *Rise Sister Rise* by Rebecca Campbell. I had seen and heard about it at various times but it never caught my attention. Then one particular day while I was visiting Glastonbury it almost leapt off the shelf at me when I was in the White Rabbit shop. Before I had even registered what I was doing I was at the till purchasing it.

Within its many pages of wisdom is one particular section with the title of "Witch Hunts". Rebecca goes on to tell us that the witch hunts lasted for 500, YES, 500 years! That shocked me so much that I am bringing it up here. The witch hunts began in the 12th century and the trials continued until well into the 17th century. These were a way of subjugating control over the masses and in particular women. The trials began in earnest from 1484 during the reign of Pope Innocent VIII when he pronounced a papal bull declaring witchcraft as heresy.

That, my lovelies, is 500 years of women living in fear. It is no wonder that we have such a strong feminist movement. This turned women against women; they were powerless and too fearful to stand up for their sisters in arms. The fear, the dread and I dare say anger was deep and widespread. The constant watching with panic filled their every waking moment of being accused or associated with witches. Think about the depth of anxiety of being tortured or killed, most frequently at the hand of a man or group of men. Men who were an idealistic fraction of fanatical and fearful men – fearful of the power of a woman!

I can feel a slow burning rage (yep, there it is again) deep in my solar plexus and a block in my throat chakra. Yes, I too am human and a work in progress.

This is part of Magdalene's work: the deep healing connected to times long past. Women can be the bitchiest of creatures and I do wonder if this ties to a fearful past: of being cast out, tortured, blamed, maimed or killed. To stand by and up for your sister in arms, your fellow woman, shoulder to shoulder, would have been terrifying. It would put you and your family in immediate danger, cost you your life and probably those near and dear. I wonder if that pain still echoes and ricochets down the female line. I do believe it does.

Divine Feminine and Masculine

There is a great deal of talk within spiritual circles about the divine feminine and divine masculine and about balancing the two. This is something that Magdalene urges us all to explore.

By balancing the divine masculine and the divine feminine within each of us we are acknowledging the divinity within all of us. We embrace the knowing that we are powerful yet gentle, brave yet quiet, supportive yet independent, logical yet intuitive. We the human race are the physical representation of this – we are duality and unity, opposites yet paired. We can possess great strength with great gentleness, authority with compassion.

We can learn to dance the perfect tango with the divine feminine and masculine held within each of us. The energies of each will ebb and flow. Knowing your dominant states will enable you to understand and balance yourself and them more easily.

In truth, as humans we are unlikely to ever achieve a perfect balance of both, but with practice and understanding when we have too much of one or the other we can actively bring a little more perspective and balance to our overall wellbeing.

Under Magdalene and her dragons' guidance we can begin the work of balancing these energies within us. Acknowledging both sides of us, bringing each into play when we need to and honouring that divinity within us.

What are Your Strongest Traits?

Spend a bit of time here thinking about your strengths and weaknesses, your masculine and feminine sides. As always there is no judgement, just simple observations. This is something to peruse and ponder upon, not go into meltdown and self-flagellation over.

You may find it helpful to list them down under feminine and masculine traits. To give you an idea, here are a few of my thoughts.

Feminine	Masculine
Intuitive	Logical
Healer	Methodical (mostly)
Organized (sometimes)	Highly organized (sometimes)
Sporadic	Practical
Flighty	Loyal

This exercise will give you an idea of where your energy sits. This is once more another huge topic that could most likely be a book on its own. So explore what it means to you and how it feels.

Magdalene and the White Lions

The White Lions are the energy of purity and power and sovereignty and grace. Their presence at the opening of the Lion's Gate shows us the way forward. The Lion's Gate portal opens around the same time as Magdalene's Feast Day on 22 July and closes on 8 August (8:8). Its opening brought through the Sapphire Ray Dragons with Magdalene at the helm.

The combination of the Sapphire Ray Dragons led by Magdalene and the White Lions at 8:8 acts as a turning point and is one of bravery. We can believe we have to toe the line in whichever form it takes or we can dig into our own innate knowledge, the higher self's well of wisdom, to find our sovereignty and voice.

The opening of the Lion's Gate gives us an expansion in consciousness and a broadening of awareness. The energies at this time are free flowing and potent. Add in the clarity of the Sapphire Ray Dragons and you will be in a position to take your life forward in ways you did not dream plausible or possible before. This is time to stand in your sovereignty and know who you are.

Lion's Gate is about integrity, wisdom and bright new energy flowing through the portal from the White Lions to expand your consciousness and awareness. You are asked to anchor the light into the world wherever you are and send it out with no attachment to outcome or agenda. This light frequency flanked by Magdalene's dragons ensures clarity, wisdom and honesty are upheld throughout the Universe. With the closing of the Lion's Gate on 8:8 you have to opportunity to experience a leap in consciousness both individually and collectively.

White Lions: A Little Background

Of course you can't have Lion's Gate without White Lions. I met the White Lions a few years ago at a Lion's Gate event held by Sue Coulson (who runs the Cosmic Classroom at the Henge Shop in Avebury) at the Sanctuary in Avebury on a rather damp and very chilly August evening. During the evening I was expecting dragons and ended up with three beautiful White Lions.

Similar to the dragons, White Lions carry energy, great wisdom and authority. Each of you will experience them as is appropriate for you in the following meditation. They and Magdalene's dragons have chosen this time to come together as we traverse and transition through these extraordinary times.

The White Lions are bringing in greater awareness for humanity's consciousness. We are being asked to hold and carry this energy. They tell me that we are all into the next phase of our spiritual evolution or, as some call it, "ascension path". This energy is one of clarity and illumination while for some it will be accountability, honesty and integrity.

It is not for us to judge the which, what, where, how and who but for each of us on the planet to hold the intention and space in our heart so that this may all take place. We are all incredibly blessed to be here now. We all have a part to play.

The mission of the White Lions is also at this moment to add bravery to our repertoire. As the world around us continues to be chaotic, the White Lions ask that we stand fast in what we know in our hearts to be true. Not what the media, friends or family tell us but our pure inner world truth, away from criticism and judgement.

Lion's Gate 8:8 Meditation

This meditation is best carried out around the time of the Lion's Gate portal, which closes on 8 August. This is a time when the energy from the stars and our galactic brethren is incredibly potent. It offers so much opportunity as it showers down and invites you to align with new DNA coding for you and your development, especially where your spiritual path is concerned.

The number 8 turned on its side is the symbol for infinity (this is also known as the lemniscate). I did a quick internet search on the infinity symbol and discovered that it began life as algebraic geometry (mathematics) in 1655 and was used by an English priest called John Wallis, although the concept of infinity goes way back to ancient Greek philosophers.

The date 8:8 offers infinite opportunity to reset, rebalance and realign with our purpose and goals of reaching for the stars. This exercise is best practised out of doors allowing you to join with the stars and the cosmos. Begin with the head and heart meditation from chapter one.

1. Visualize your energy anchoring deep into the Earth into the crystal grids via a bright golden disc at your feet.
2. With each breath allow your energy to expand up and out, taking it as far out into the cosmos as you can reach.
3. As you do so you touch the edges of the Sapphire Ray Dragons and they observe you as you draw its bright vibrant colour down into your energy field. They will support you if you require it.
4. As you fill with the sovereign energy you are joined by the White Lions. They are regal, beautiful and powerful. The White Lions invite you to fully embrace your bravery, truth and authenticity. Your time of playing small has come to an end.
5. The White Lions invite you to stand tall with them, to be seen and to be heard. Your time and possibilities are infinite.

An Invitation from Magdalene

You can use the Sapphire Ray Dragons to clear the ever present divisiveness that is separating humanity to heal timelines and trauma and the collective pain of our great, great grandmothers of long ago.

Magdalene invites you to connect with her and her dragons. She says that connecting to the energy and power of the Sapphire Ray Dragons lifts our collective energy above the humdrum and the drama that plays out all around us. Remember that whatever is going on now in your own personal orbit or outside in the world at large, it is all perfect and as it is all meant to be right now. Actively activating the Sapphire Ray Dragons enables you to embrace a more balanced approach to life – your life.

DRAGON TALK

Magdalene says:

"*See and be seen, hear and be heard, fight the good fight but not to your detriment. Discernment is needed more than ever now.*

"*As women you forget you are the master creators. Over recent years women (and men) have begun the process of reclaiming their power; you no longer need to accept being less than.*

"*Now you reclaim your birthright and bring your collective wisdom to the table.*

"*The Sapphire Rays are here to unite women collectively in my name across the worlds. Accept your own divinity through every stage of your life.*

"*You can stand shoulder to shoulder yet be unique and individual.*

"*Forge your path with your Sapphire dragons at your side.*

"*Carry your sword of wisdom wisely, with integrity and clarity.*

"*Woman, you are the power.*

"We were feared for our power and intuition. Your work now entails healing the wounds which divided us. Our ancestors connected to the flowing waters, to the waxing and waning moon. They understood creation in all its forms, the cycle of life, death and rebirth, and they were cast as witches and heathens.

"Women knew the power of their monthly flow, and how it knitted and wove its way into the fabric of their daily life.

"Women are today as they have always been, the conduit and life balancer. They are the embodiment of unconditional love, and this is power, real power. Men were afraid of a woman's capacity for it, along with the ability to forgive.

"Knowing what has been done cannot be changed, but the pain connected to it can be transformed. That is sovereignty."

Remember when working with dragons that nothing is in isolation nor coincidental. The Sapphire Ray and the dragons within it are multifaceted and carry what we need as a collective right now. They show us the breaking down of old systems, outmoded beliefs with authority and traditions being challenged, but more importantly the need of integrity, truth and illumination.

With great change first comes upheaval and then out of the chaotic upheaval the likes of Magdalene and her blue ray dragons bring the stabilising factor. The desire to stand fast in your beliefs is a noble one; please note this is not to be rigid nor "dog in the manger". Just because you have always believed or done something a certain way does not mean it has to stay that way.

Flexibility and adaptability come to mind with the Sapphire Ray Dragons and Magdalene. That deep knowing of when to push and when to hold steady. We will continue to encounter challenges and shakeups for a while yet. All of this means that we can call on Magdalene and her dragons to help steady our respective ships as we navigate choppy waters.

You may find that you would like to embark on your work with Magdalene at the time of the Feast of Magdalene, which is on 22 July, or at the time of the Lion's Gate which opens around the Feast of Magdalene and closes on 8 August (8:8).

Magdalene Empowerment Meditation

1. Visualize Magdalene coming toward you. She is sitting astride a magnificent Sapphire Ray Dragon. Streaming out behind her forming a V shape are six other blue dragons.
2. Magdalene stops in front of you with the dragons forming a half circle around you. You feel yourself being observed by the dragons and have a sense of Magdalene's power and deep compassion. She knows how powerful you truly are and that this power can feel intimidating. She is here with the dragons to remind you that you have nothing to fear. You are meant to be a powerful sovereign soul at this time.

3. A bolt of blue light is sent to you from Magdalene's hands. You can accept it or return it. As you watch the light, it grows in size and she invites you to step into it. As you do so, the dragons form a complete circle around you and Magdalene. They ask if you wish to transcend all space and time to heal the pain of the preceding generations of your grandmothers and great grandmothers, empowering you to pass the energy of sovereignty and wisdom along the female line so you may know the wisdom of their secrets.

4. Once you let the dragons know your decision, you see a bolt of light coming from them. You then have a sense of connection to your female ancestors as many generations back as you wish to go. You may get glimpses (or knowings) of their joy and pain, their wisdom and enlightenment. Here under the guidance of the dragons and Magdalene, this pain can be transcended, the wounds negated. The lessons are complete and their work is finished. This is the time for women to step into their own divinity and power under the guidance of Magdalene in the presence of the Sapphire Ray Dragons.

5. The dragons as one breathe blue fire and light down through your ancestral line. The energy then returns back to you along your line, clearing, healing and releasing as it passes from one generation to the next – mother to daughter, grandmother to granddaughter, aunt to niece, sister to sister, cousin to cousin. The time has now come to close the chapter and release the pain for it has no place in you today or tomorrow. Magdalene invites you to accept the women who went before you; to accept their love, knowledge and joy for they are a part of you and your female line.

6. If you are ready to embark upon this task Magdalene and the dragons will pass you this power, great wisdom and knowledge. If you choose to accept it, it will ensure your energetic system carries the blueprint of your existence, for you to take this work forward for generations. It will become a part of your essence for that is who you are in your female line.

7. Spend some time allowing the energy of the Sapphire Rays to integrate. Allow this energy to settle into your system, to carry you forwards in the days, weeks, months and years ahead.

8. Once the energy has settled into the core of your being you feel its power and potency shoot up into the skies, to the stratosphere and out into the deep heavens, back down again, coming in through your crown chakra, down through your body as it anchors deeply into the heart of Mother Earth.

This is a powerful mediation to work with and can bring a lot to the surface. As always under the dragons' guidance go gently with yourself. You may need a few days to process this particular meditation, so eat lightly with plenty of fresh fruit and vegetables, drink plenty of water and allow yourself to just be.

DRAGON TALK

I asked Magdalene about the qualities of the Sapphire Ray Dragons and she had this to say:

"By being enveloped in the Sapphire Ray you are being offered the opportunity to reset your energy and focus. This can be on any or every level. Blue is referred to as the colour of communication, and the sapphire blue colour of these particular dragons is associated with royalty. That deep yet bright blue. So sovereignty is brought forward here, the power, truth and integrity, and honourability.

"The opportunity to reset and adjust course is very profound with these dragons. They and this opportunity offer you the chance to shift gear, change direction, leave behind what does not serve your highest learning or presence in this body you currently inhabit."

Invoking the Sapphire Ray Dragons for Change

1. Visualize the Sapphire Ray Dragons encircling you.
2. As one, they fill your aura with blue sapphire light. Feel this settle into your body (throat or third eye chakra) knowing you own your truth, power and sovereignty.
3. Know you own your light which nothing can dim. You are connected to the Sapphire Ray and the Magdalene dragons now.

The Sapphire Rays contain alignment coding that is unique to each person. The codes carry exactly what they require at that time for spiritual advancement, alignment to the soul contract and bravery to step up and out.

DRAGON TIP

➤ *REMEMBER YOU ARE A SOVEREIGN BEING.*
➤ *WORKING WITH THE DRAGONS CAN BE TRANSFORMATIONAL.*

CHAPTER

12

Galactic Dragons

The next three chapters all work in tandem. It has been a challenge to try to break this down so it follows some form of order as there are many crossovers. But the dragons have guided my way.

My hope is that the following pages all make sense to you as the reader. The dragons like to stretch and push us through our comfort zones, to think outside our normal everyday restraints.

The Galactic Dragons' task in the Universe is that of a peacekeeping role. Their official title is the Galactic Peacekeeping Force. Needing to understand this a little better I returned once more to the dragons for more details.

Below is what they told me, including a dragon slap.

DRAGON TALK

"It was about time you asked that particular question, we have been waiting for you.

"The Galactic Dragons are the guardians of stars, galaxies and the universes.

"*Our work is to keep the balance, the equilibrium across the galaxies and the universes. Battles used to rage and all sides lost, for in truth there is never a winner in war – everyone loses. Our duty now is to watch over the peace to maintain it. We dragons can actually be quite diplomatic when we need to be.*

"*There is much beyond your solar system you as a child of Earth do not understand. There are multiple universes, solar systems, suns, moons and planetary systems. All this has a level of order which we maintain with others such as the star beings and the Galactic Light Force.*

"*We hold and are the guardians of what you think of as the keys and codes to ascension. The codes are light information which support the Earth and your spiritual evolution. This is all in Divine Order. Nothing is separate;, we are all interconnected, even the other galaxies and universes with divine timing.*

"*The codes and keys in particular refer to the light code information being released to those on Earth, to those who are able to hold, anchor and activate the light grids which you call dragon song lines (we like this name you have given them) on your planet.*

"*The light codes are released during particular points throughout your calendar year into your stratosphere. These come into your Earth's orbit via the light refraction portals where you connect to them.*

"These dates are the 11:11 Gateway and 8:8 Lion's Gate amongst others."

The Galactic Dragons have another role as well. They are the overseers of all the energy portals that bring in the light codes at particular points throughout our calendar year. They also enjoy and connect with sound. Their frequency is that of the gongs and crystal bowls in particular. I dare say you will find other sounds and frequencies too, which they align to if you choose to work with them.

You have probably realized now that there are many crossovers with the dragons, such as the White Lions of Lion's Gate with Magdalene and her dragons, Atlantis and the Grand Masters, and so it is with the Galactic Dragons. Their connection is with the star beings, crystal skulls, whether dragon, alien or star elfin crystal energies, the constellations, galaxies and dimensions and Mary Magdalene and the Dragons of the Land!

All dragons respond to crystals as these too carry a frequency whether in their raw form, carved or polished. The common crystal for gaining a greater dragon connection is quartz. This can be any of the quartz family: clear, rose, smoky and the aqua aura quartzes.

DRAGON TALK

Within our spiritual circles we hear a fair amount of talk about dimensions, galaxies, Atlantis and more, so I asked the dragons for some straightforward clarity on the matter.

This is what they gave me:

"Atlantis and the Galactic Dragons are connected as that is where their advanced information came from for Atlantis. For clarity Atlantis was in another dimension to the one you live in."

The dragons went on to tell me that our galaxy with all its planets, star systems and black holes makes up our Universe as we know it. Beyond this there are further black holes, galaxies and star systems.

Dimensions on the other hand are beyond this Universe and other universes in an energetic sense. Places like Atlantis, Lemuria, the Pleiades and the Acturians are interdimensional and not of our galaxy. Each of these has "localized satellite stations" within our Universe and galactic dimension, but their original home is a different galaxy or dimension. All somewhat mind blowing information!

The light beings and dragons guide our way. They aid and support our spiritual evolution, light body and personal matrix work and the work we do for the planet and humanity on the matrix of Earth, crystal beds and the Universe. This work is limitless and infinite. The dragons show us that nothing is in isolation in our world – everything is connected and interconnected. All dragon work is vast but the Galactic Dragons take it to a whole new level of expansion.

DRAGON TALK

I was given the following channelled message by a star being from Andromeda:

"Sacred geometry is the building blocks of your world, and this is the part the dragons played, hence their love of it. It is the fabric of your world.

"The shape of a shell, a snowflake or ice particle, sand even, they had a hand in it all – well, paw or claw really. [I hear a chuckle here as they giggle at their own words.]

"Take time to look at the leaves on the trees, the shape of a petal on a flower. This is the magic and the manifest of the dragons."

In essence the Galactic Dragons oversee and protect the light portals that carry all the information and light codes we need as a species and for our planet to continue to heal, grow and evolve. This supports our spiritual evolution and in turn ascension. Without the light coding we would all stagnate with regards to leaps in science, spiritual advancement and recalling memories of ancient times, whether ancestral or past life. Our connection with the star beings would either be lost or certainly less secure.

The Galactic Dragons are responsible for guiding us in our work with DNA upgrades, carrying and connecting to the fifth dimension and above, supporting and clearing our own light body as well as those surrounding our planet. I talk more about this in the following chapter.

We do not have the same kind of connection with the Galactic Dragons as we do with the other clans. But they will work with us, usually in the form of giving information that we need rather than the teaching and lessons that we receive from the other dragons. I think of them as an information portal. A little like the World Wide Web but dragon style.

Within my deck under the heading of the Galactic Dragons, we have four dragons. These are Luna, Lord Kuthumi, Crystal and Actramis.

DRAGON TALK

I met the dragon Luna back in 2017. In addition to her message contained within the guidebook of my deck, she had this to say to me:

"I work with and represent the weather, the tide and the storms, the power of the raging torrents of water. I have the power and ability to raise or to calm the storms. Those which rage within or outside of you. I am the powerhouse of energy bringing about the fury and blast of a tornado to the trickling springs and gently flowing waters of a shallow brook."

This dual aspect dragon is a powerful ally to have by your side in tumultuous times. She can wreak havoc as she blasts through walls and barriers and can just as gently carry you through. Balance is a precious commodity and one that we all seek. So after the storm comes the calm. You can call on Luna during the time of a storm, whether these are literal storms or emotional ones. Luna is a great dragon to connect with; she is particularly potent during the full moon or the new moon.

Invoking Luna

Calling on Luna at tumultuous times can be incredibly insightful. There are two very simple ways to do this.

1. Visualize Luna in front of you and simply talk to her like you would a close and trusted friend. Share with her what concerns you, where you would like her help and what requires calming or redesigning in your life. Listen for her wisdom and messages with your body and inner knowing. You may see images or hear words or she may give you a knowing that you feel is true and right.
2. With your journal in front of you, visualize Luna in your mind's eye and begin to write whatever comes to mind. Feel your way with it.

The final way to work with Luna in difficult times is to ask her to be with you while you work through and traverse the challenges you are facing. She will be your constant companion if you ask her. She will nudge and guide you if you listen for it, often in surprising ways.

Connecting with the Galactic Dragons

Each of us carries the template (or blueprint) of wholeness, uniqueness and spiritual completeness that make us, us. By working with the dragons and in particular the Galactic Dragons and other archetypes we are simply using or more accurately reawakening those properties within our blueprint.

We call upon the qualities of these archetypes to remind us, realign us and reprogramme or plug back in the pieces we have forgotten. These aspects of self are held within the core of our very being, whether you consider this to be your soul, DNA or something else altogether. It does not matter what you call it or believe it to be, what matters is the work that you do.

If you would like to specifically work with Galactic Dragons, there is a meditation coming up to help you on your way. Do not be surprised if you end up connecting to and conversing with a star being. This has happened to me.

The deeper you ground and connect with the heart of Mother Earth, the higher you can reach energy wise. You may like to use the extended chakra meditation from chapter four to support your connection to both the Earth and the Galactic Dragons. Once you have carried out the extended chakra meditation, you can continue with the meditation below.

A Galactic Meditation

1. When you feel ready, ask the Galactic Dragon that is perfect for you and your journey to join you.
2. Use this time to explore the galaxies with them, ask questions and fly freely with your new winged friend. Follow your intuition and higher knowing. Seek answers and question deeply. The dragons thoroughly enjoy sharing their wisdom. They will have much to show and share with you.
3. When you feel you are ready, begin to bring your awareness back into this reality. Remember as always to thank the energies and dragons you have worked with for their guidance, wisdom, knowledge and protection.
4. When you are back remember to close the chakras down from crown to root.

Working with high frequency energies can leave you feeling a tad spacey, so make sure you take time to write up your experiences, reground if you need to, have a glass of water and allow yourself time to adjust back to the denser energies of Earth and our three-dimensional existence.

Galactic Work Energies

The Galactic Dragons guide our work with the light portals, and guide us in anchoring the incoming light codes and its frequency into the planet; this is spiritual evolution in action. In short, the Galactic's light up and lead us in our spiritual quest. They oversee the opening of the portal energies and guide us in anchoring DNA recoding into our energetic systems, enabling us to align with our greatest spiritual life and potential here on Earth.

Dragons of Light

The Galactic Dragons' role is vast and far reaching. The other dragons under the heading of Galactic Dragons are those of the Dragons of Light. They have two different titles or names they go under: the Dragons of Light is their collective name but they can also be described as the Helix Ray Dragons. Each of them connects with a specific colour and supports our spiritual quest as well as Gaia in her spiritual evolution.

Each set of Dragons of Light carry specific healing energy. Here I will take you through working with the Golden Helix Ray Dragons. Do not mix up the Helix Ray Dragons with Magdalene's Sapphire Ray Dragons as these are different dragons!

In late 2020 I was fully introduced to the Dragons of Light. In early 2021 we saw completion of a cycle that began 2,221 years ago as humanity entered the Piscean age. Over the coming months and I am sure years we will witness the last vestiges of the old energy leave Earth and our systems. We will be guided to thank the previous time frame for all its experiences for us personally, our ancestors and all those who came before us as the portal closes fully.

At the beginning of 2021 we witnessed the opening of the light refraction portal – the birthing of its existence if you like. The birthing of this new energy will continue to build and grow as we move through the next 2,221 years. It is multifaceted and carries many levels of knowledge, healing and light within it.

You will not do all this work in one go. It will be a continuous journey of discovery, healing and understanding as you deepen your spiritual connection to yourselves, each other, the dragons and the Universe, including working with the Helix Ray Dragons.

Those of you embarking upon this journey in the early stages will be at the forefront of holding and anchoring its frequency and supporting the planet, plants, animals, insects and humans as you all continue your evolutionary and spiritual journeys for all the future generations that follow in your footsteps.

The Dragons of Light are drawing down the light codes within the light refractions portal direct from the source allowing you to access them with ease at a rate that is right for you. This clears blocks of all kinds, anything from emotional pain, this life and previous ones to releasing binding chains and ancient patterning held within your DNA.

Their other role is one of activating your personal spiritual DNA coding. This is far reaching and covers all aspects of our humanness and spiritual potential.

The light code work that is carried out over the coming months and years is not just for today. It is for each and every one of us on a personal and spiritual level. It is also for the whole of humanity and the planet.

Over the next few pages you will build a stronger relationship and deeper understanding of all the Dragons of Light as they introduce you to the new energy they are bringing in. This will continue to build and grow as you tap into it and use it. I am sure it will also evolve and grow as our collective spiritual understanding expands.

The dragons nudged me to remind you of some things that they have taught me over the years. Many of us experience everything including our spiritual side externally. We unconsciously see it as separate from us whereas it is actually our spiritual nature. It is who and what we are. We are not outside it and nor is it separate to us. Everything is connected, as you know.

As humans we mistakenly "think" too much and believe we can think ourselves out of trouble, pain, confusion and more. But our biggest mistake is that we think we are our minds and our brains. And unconsciously our brain, thoughts and minds control us.

This is not the time nor the place to get into the workings of this, the hows or the whys. What this does do though is show us that we are naturally heart-based creatures. Just look to the animals who share your life. They are forgiving, trusting and loving whatever their experiences at the human hand. They love, give and want to be with us as they are all heart-based.

Like our furry four-legged friends we are meant to be heart-based but have forgotten this. If we stop to connect, we can be heart-based too. For this is where we truly heal from and where our real truth resides.

As much as anything, this entire book has been to guide you with your dragons to remember who you are as a heart-based spiritual being. For this is the true essence of love. And that is the gift of the dragons, and in particular the Dragons of Light.

If you have followed me from my early days, you will know that dragons are not fond of the word "love". It is a human habit to say, "Oh, I love that dress on you, love that colour, car, perfume, bag ... " This compounds our externalisation of the word and meaning of love. It gets used to externalize – i.e. we love things and these things are outside of us, therefore re-enforcing the separation existence we live in and create.

By doing this we miss the word's deeper understanding. "Love" has lost its depth, its real meaning. For the dragons, it can't be replaced by one singular word; they view love as a mix of words such as grace, gratitude, hope, compassion and so on. To really understand this we need to learn to drop into our heart and experience love (for ourselves first) in its purest sense. When practised regularly your dragons will guide you to be more balanced in your emotions, thoughts and actions as by now you have experienced this with the head and heart meditation (chapter one).

By now I suspect your awareness will have shifted and you are beginning to recognize when you are not in your heart (and have returned to your head) so I hope you are making time in your daily life to drop back in to it. When you begin to live life with an awareness of a heart-centred space, you are learning who you are. Fears, doubts, anxiety, etc. begin to drop away as you gain far greater personal awareness and your true beauty and expression begin to flourish. This opens you all to a kaleidoscope of opportunities to grow, heal, develop and of course gain a deeper relationship with our dragon kin. In essence it teaches us to be more mindful.

Practising being heart-based over time brings about a number of changes. This can be a bumpy ride as you release the old and embrace the new. No one ever said that living the human spiritual existence here in this three dimensional world was a walk in the park. This is why we have dragons at our side.

Over time you will find yourself listening to your body and your inner knowing more and more. You may find old patterns such as judgements dropping away, having clearer personal boundaries and moving on from relationships of all kinds that do not align with you.

To carry this energy effectively dragons will guide you in clearing emotional blocks, wounds or pain, whether physical or emotional. Much physical pain originates as repressed or unacknowledged and unhealed emotional pain. This may be old or recent, it does not matter which. To hold the light and to carry out future work with them, this work is required first.

We are on the cusp of change with the new energies coming through. The dragons vibrate with the frequency of the Universe. By practising the head and heart meditation regularly you too will begin to vibrate at the new frequency.

How the Heart Meditation Came into Being

The head and heart meditation that you have been using all the way through this book was given to me while I was channelling the Dragons of Light Workshop in readiness for the 2021 workshop. As I suspect you have discovered, this meditation grounds you so deeply if you practise it properly. Your scattered energies, both thoughts and auric energy, draw back to you and strengthen your auric field. It is like have a shield around you and is quite potent.

To experience the following meditation with the Dragons of Light, you will need to begin by using the head and heart meditation and then continue with the practice below.

Connecting with the Dragons of Light

1. Staying with the breath draw your awareness inwards and shift your consciousness to your heart. As you do this you will become aware of your heart chakra expanding. The dragons call this "dropping into your heart". Feel the expansion of your heart chakra from the inside as you drop deeper and deeper into your heart at a conscious level. You will begin to feel warmth from the heart flow through your body.
2. In your mind's eye see yourself within a sacred or ancient site. This can be anywhere in the world, such as Uluru, Machu Picchu, any of the stone circles or ancient groves, wherever you are drawn to. You may

find yourself flitting about until you find the right spot for you energetically. Go with it, staying deep within your heart and your breath. Wherever you decide will be perfect and you will be guided by your higher knowing.

3. Once you have settled feel your connection to the land there. Feel its ancientness as you connect deeply with it.

4. In the periphery of your vision there is a glowing whiteish light. Turn to face it. As you watch, it builds to form a beautiful arch filled with illuminous light. You can feel its energy.

5. Once the arch has reached its peak, the Dragons of Light come pouring through it, flying toward you and forming a large circle around you. They are iridescent, sparkling, shining and HUGE. You can feel their frequency as the ground beneath you vibrates slightly. The dragons spread their wings, with the tips overlapping, and the energy increases further.

6. Hold your focus at your heart. Slowly allow your consciousness to expand. Feel yourself connect with the energy of the dragons. As you do so the Dragons of Light draw down the light refractions. Feel the energy the dragons have brought forward and allow your entire being to become accustomed to this new frequency.

7. Slowly begin to turn within the circle of dragons, feeling for a connection with one in particular. Once the connection is made the dragon steps forward and lowers their head in greeting. You connect forehead to forehead and they silently ask if you are ready to do this work. The remaining dragons move together, completing the circle once more, holding the space for both of you.

8. Your chosen dragon raises themselves to their full magnificent height and draws some of the light energy toward them. The energy holds the light codes for your own personal healing – emotional, physical,

mental and spiritual, whatever it is that you need at this time.

9. Your dragon guides you to open your heart, expanding it from the inside to allow its energy to reach toward them. From here the dragons will guide you to draw in the light and the coding in through your heart chakra for any personal healing work you wish to carry out. Stay with your heart; notice any thoughts that intrude then take your focus back to your breath back and your heart once more.

Allow 10 to 15 minutes for this work to take place.

10. Immerse yourself in the energy; feel it fill and flow in through your heart. Listen to your own inner knowing, staying with a heart-centred awareness. Your dragon will guide you.

11. Gradually the intensity of the light begins to dim. The flow slows down. You now have all the information you need at this time. Your dragon looks directly at you and drops their head to yours once more.

12. As they lift their head the remaining dragons lower their wings and move aside, allowing their friend to join their ranks once more. As one, they turn toward the now fading light of the portal. Their work is complete for now.

13. You stand and watch as the dragons take flight and disappear through the portal of light. As the last tail flicks through, the portal closes.

14. Take a few moments to thank the previous time frame for all its experiences for you personally, your ancestors and all those who came before you as the portal closes behind them.

Spend some time in the quiet. Staying in your heart, do a full body scan, physical and energetic, to see how you feel. And in your own time bring your awareness back. Wiggle your fingers and toes, stretch and open your eyes.

Once you have fully integrated this energy and done any work you need to around your own personal journey you will be able to carry the light codes more deeply. In turn you will have the opportunity to work with the Dragons of Light to carry out the healing of the matrix and grids for the rest of humanity. This is covered in the last chapter.

Over the coming days and weeks I invite you to keep up with your journaling on a regular basis as you will witness shifts on many levels. Some may be small, subtle nuances; others could be on a much larger scale as you integrate with the new energies. It would also be a good idea to consciously keep a clear energy system by using the violet flame decree (chapter seven). This is high frequency work and calls for us all to carry a clear energy.

Golden Ray Helix Dragons

Here we connect with Actramis, the dragon of the seventh dimensional golden ray helix. The work you carry out with the Galactic Dragons and in particular the Golden Ray Helix Dragons will be among the most important that you do. This is work for the planet.

Just as we are on a journey of spiritual evolution so is Mother Gaia who is a living, breathing entity. As we evolve so does she by anchoring the light codes held in the Helix for Earth's evolution. Here is where the true alchemy takes place.

Each coloured helix holds a series of light codes for the planet and for us. As we work on healing the grids, Gaia releases the light patterns for us all to access as a collective via the song lines. These of course will be most potent at sacred sites.

Those of us who are ready to absorb the helix energy will take it out into the world to share with others as appropriate. We are here to share the wisdom and knowledge of Gaia and the golden helix. I will cover all of this in more detail in the coming chapters.

The dragons invite you to help create a new paradigm on Earth. When talking with the dragons about this energy they told me:

DRAGON TALK

"It is for you not only to remember the ancient wisdoms of the Galactics of which we are all a part but also for you to remember who you are in essence, your true innate spiritual nature.

"Many of these things and attributes have been forgotten over the millennia and the golden helix offers you the opportunity to anchor these new codes into the very being of your DNA, and that work my friend is the work of the Dragons of Light.

"The Dragons of Light and the Ray Dragons are interchangeable names. In essence the Dragons of Light from a colouration point of view are a translucent white, and some see them as rainbow coloured. The Helix Ray Dragons are specific colours of ruby, gold, emerald or platinum."

There are a number of ways to work with the Golden Helix Dragons from the Dragons of Light. You can anchor the Golden Helix Ray by drawing it down from above, by bringing it down through your crown chakra into your light body and allowing it to settle wherever feels appropriate to you. This may change each time you practise this meditation, depending on whichever chakra is appropriate at the time for your development and what you are working on at that time. It commonly settles into the solar plexus, but will go to whichever chakra requires it.

Working with the Golden Ray Helix Dragons

There are a couple of ways to work with the Golden Helix Dragons. This work is ultimately about our individual and collective awakening. Each of you will receive exactly what you need and require for the next step of your spiritual journey.

The Golden Helix energy can be drawn down and anchored into the heart of Mother Earth to release the codes the planet needs at the time. You can also work with Magdalene and the Sapphire Ray Dragons. I did this recently with a client during a healing session and it was quite unexpected.

As I was working and connecting with the universal healing energy of the dragons, I saw my client encased in the blue of Magdalene and had a sense of the Sapphire Dragons surrounding her. As I was marvelling at the beautiful blue of the Sapphire Ray energy I saw what appeared to be golden rain drops pouring into her aura. As these rain drops settled into the aura they turned into tiny helixes, the spiralling golden light of the golden helix.

This particular exercise transcends space and time. It carries upgrades that you need now, as well as releasing you from old karmic patterning and ancestral obligation that you no longer need to carry.

Light Coding with the Golden Helix

The light coding of the golden helix consists of light strands of renewed DNA coding. Working with the Galactic Dragons to access the frequency of the golden helix aligns you to integrate and activate the golden light helix into every cell of your being. DNA recoding supports our spiritual path and growth exponentially. It puts us onto the superfast highway of spiritual evolution.

Golden Helix for the Planet

While I was working on the final edit of this book, the dragons were nagging me to go to Avebury. As ever I initially ignored them, resolutely digging in my heels as I had a deadline to meet and a day playing in Avebury was out of the question.

Eventually they put the brakes on my writing and editing and refused to cooperate with me until I took notice. I was given instructions to work with the golden helix and the Dragons of Light.

On my way down there it dawned on me that the date was 11.01.22 – two master numbers. It was a wet, foggy and pretty miserable day but Avebury was quiet, so perfect to do what they asked of me. Also on the way down I realized in my rush to get out the door that I had not picked up my dragon skulls so I was kicking myself for my haste!

Before I set to work I popped into the Henge Shop to wish everyone "Happy New Year" as I had not been down there for quite some time. While I was there, Phillipe who owns the Henge Shop gifted me a beautiful ruby and zionite carved palm stone dragon. I was honestly gobsmacked and incredibly grateful! How very perfect; this was why mine had stayed at home.

My intention of working in the Avenue soon shifted as the dragons guided me. As I walked out into the stones to feel where I would be working, I noticed a white thread of light was travelling from each stone to the sun circle. The entire Henge has energy lines criss-crossing it like a spider's web. Energy was travelling from each megalith to the sun circle and back again. Avebury has its own web of light!

The dragons guided me to the centre of the sun circle where I was to call in the Dragons of Light from each direction. At each point I felt compelled to use a different set of words: "Dragon of Light, join me to clear, to heal, to rebalance, align, realign, repair, cleanse and support the dragon song lines."

I felt the Dragons of Light surround the whole of Avebury and collectively they breathed pure white cleansing, balancing and healing fire into the centre of the sun circle. Once this was complete it was the turn of the Golden Ray Helix Dragons. I did wonder if this would be energy overload, but I was told to continue so I did.

The next set of work was to be carried out by the Devil's Chair (some call it the Goddess Chair). This is the main entrance to Avebury where processions would have come though from the Avenue to the sun circle.

I was to stand between these two huge megaliths and anchor the golden helix light into the Earth. The intention of this is to support the Henge and Gaia but more than that they will release their secrets at the appropriate time to spiritual seekers. The perfect place to work with and anchor the golden helix into the planet is outside in nature, ideally at a sacred site and ancient historical lands. The reason behind this, the dragons tell me, is so that it can reach more people. Those who are ready will feel it, recognize it and welcome it in. Of course this can be done remotely if access to the site of your choice is not possible.

Golden Helix for Humanity and the Planet Visualization

Centre and ground yourself in a spot where you can sit quietly without being too disturbed.

1. Ask the Golden Helix Dragons to join you. You sense them form a circle around you and as they do so they spread their wings with their tips gently overlapping.
2. Above you, you see the swirling of the golden helix. Visualize it spiralling down toward you until it touches the ground just in front of you. As it does so a bright golden whirlpool of energy opens in the ground allowing the helix spiral to flow down into the Earth and be held there or released. This will be released by Gaia when she is ready.

DRAGON TIP

WE ARE NOT OUTSIDE OF OR SEPARATE TO OUR SPIRITUALNESS. IT IS US – WE ARE IT.

CHAPTER

13

Light Body and the Merkabah

When it comes to spiritually advanced work one of the first things the dragons realized when they began working with us is that we were not as spiritually adept or advanced as they or we thought. We were not quite ready for their powerful energy.

They then understood that we as humans needed to learn a lot. And I mean a LOT! We needed (and still do) to learn to heal and take responsibility for ourselves: our actions, thoughts and emotions and who and what we are. From there we needed to learn to stand up and speak up for ourselves. Stand in our power and authenticity.

We need to learn to be brave and to honour us as humans and value all our emotions. We also need to learn to be more present, to let go of fear, guilt, frustration and more. All of this is a work in progress for the entirety of mankind. But you and I are getting better at it. Now that we are gradually understanding all of this and taking the steps to heal, the next phase is coming through. This is work that the dragons really want to do with us. It is spiritual evolution and many call it "ascension".

Ascension has been talked about a lot in spiritual circles, but the dragons tell me that we have missed the point slightly. We have been trying to build our spiritual evolution on sand.

We have been too much "love and light". To truly grow on all levels we need to understand that we are all shades of light and dark. Our job is to accept and understand this.

When we consciously and actively begin meditating to keep our chakra and auric fields clear, by default we carry more light within our physical and energy systems. Part of the dragons' task of working with us is to guide, enable and oversee the process of our personal light body upgrade. They are guiding us to be a clear channel; to be light and bright within our entire energetic system.

As you work through this process you may find yourself removing all kinds of toxins from your life. This can be anything from people, situations, other people's dramas, certain foods, habits, caffeine, etc.

The dragons have come to guide you in your spiritual development and encourage you to awaken your light bodies and ignite your own Merkabah. Their aim is that we become walking spiritual masters in our lifetime. We have much work to do. Over the years they have guided and given me parts of the puzzle. Gradually it has all come together to form the picture and guidance you now hold in your hands.

Your Light Body

The main part of your light body is made up of your chakras and aura. Another part is your personal energy flow. You can think of it as your chi or prana. Although for me it feels more like our essence, the purest and brightest version of us. In short, our soul.

This is your connection to the Universe and the Earth. Your essence is made up of your entire energy field and through it you communicate with the dragons. It is always in constant movement and always connected to all that is.

Your aura acts as a shield to your personal space and energy and is always picking up the subtle energies of the world around you, and when required amplifying them.

Your chakras are your own personal language, the interpreters if you like, or even the voices of your personal connection to all that is. In many ways they act as translators between you and the rest of your energy system. And all of this is brought together via your personal energy blueprint and essence. This energy of essence keeps everything moving within your chakras and aura. Its job is to hold everything in balance, supporting a clear energy field and chakra flow.

The dragons showed you how to begin the upgrade of your light bodies using frequency, with the chakra upgrade covered in chapter four. That was part one of your light body. Part two is the Merkabah. Your task now is to activate your own Merkabah, connecting to your personal light matrix and that of the planet. At some point, now lost in the eons of time, we were connected to it but almost certainly not here on this planet.

Golden Helix Light Body

The golden helix offers you the opportunity to draw down golden light coding that will enhance all your spiritual practices as guided by the Golden Dragons of the seventh dimensional golden ray of wisdom and knowledge. It allows you to tap into this great wisdom, for this energy comes directly from the source and is brought into your awareness through the dragons that look after it.

Through working with the golden helix you have the opportunity to clear and upgrade at a deep cellular (DNA) level. And as always with the dragons, where more light is thrown it will undoubtedly bring to the surface more shadow themes to be worked through.

Our bodies are designed to carry and transmit light. We are designed to be light, not only in essence of energy but of soul too. We are here to walk lightly upon our Earth, to carry a light touch and to light the way for others to follow. We, you and I, are here to be light workers. Light worker is not a favoured term of the dragons, but in this instance they have allowed it to be used to make their point!

This is why you chose to incarnate now. You are lighting and leading the way so others may follow in your footsteps. The golden helix takes your healing and light body to another level, and it is working with this energy that skyrockets your spiritual evolution.

Anchoring the golden helix through your light body is some of the most sacred work you will do. Drawing down and working with the golden helix within your own energy system will enhance your spiritual practice exponentially. This work is not done and dusted in one day. It is work that you will most likely revisit on a fairly regular basis. How often you choose to work with the Golden Dragons is entirely up to you, but as a guide I would suggest weekly is a good place to start.

Golden Helix Visualization

1. Ask the Golden Helix Dragons to join you.
2. You sense them form a circle around you, and as they do so they spread their wings with their tips gently overlapping.
3. Above you, you see the swirling of the golden helix. This is your own personal golden helix for your growth and for healing spiritual evolution.
4. Draw in down through your crown chakra, then through each energy centre until you feel the familiar click as it connects into the appropriate chakra for you now.
5. Once the golden helix has settled into your chosen energy centre, feel its energy fill that chakra. Once that chakra is full, feel the golden light flow into each

chakra in turn, filling and overflowing until your entire body and aura is full of golden flowing light.

6. Allow the golden helix to flow down through your root chakra and connect with each of your Earth chakras in turn, anchoring and holding this energy for you, grounding it deeply.

Now that you have anchored your personal golden helix you can work with it with intention. This can be for healing; in particular for the clearing and balancing of your ancestral line, releasing karma and karmic debts, releasing you from karmic vows and deep personal healing. Any intentional work you do around this with your golden helix will be guided by the Golden Ray Dragons.

The golden helix and Golden Ray Dragons will also work with you on clearing blocks you may have around abundance and flow. This is challenging work as it brings to the fore layers of resistance, fears, doubts, guilt and more.

Once more the dragons show us how everything is connected.

Working with Intention

When it comes to working with the dragons and intention the first thing is to be extremely clear at this level what you wish to work on. Now is a good time to return to your journal as you formulate the wording for your intention. You will have done this a few times by now I hope so you know the format.

1. Once you have the words that feel right, connect into your golden helix energy with your chakra system (body, Earth and higher ones) and invoke the Golden Helix Dragons to join you.
2. State your intention to them, asking that they guide your work.
3. Set your intention free, visualizing as the golden helix energy flows with it, clearing, healing, balancing, releasing and more.

The Merkabah

The Merkabah is made up of two tetrahedron shapes (three-dimensional pyramid shapes) intersecting each other, one facing point upwards and the other point downwards. These then spin in opposite directions. The vibrations of the spin in turn create a complete circle of energy around you. We are back to sacred geometry once again!

Merkabah has ancient connections and is actually Hebrew for "chariot", a vehicle for travel. It appears to have begun life in early Jewish mysticism with numerous mentions in the Bible although my feeling is that it has been around for far longer. The word Merkabah consists of three words: Mer meaning light, Ka meaning spirit and Bah meaning body.

The Galactic Dragons can travel vast distances and whiz in and out of dimensions, galaxies and universes in the blink of an eye. When your Merkabah is activated and aligned with your light body, greater opportunities deepen your dragon connection, in particular with the Galactic Dragons, and you can travel with them if you choose to.

Merkabah Activation Visualization

The following meditation introduces you to activating your Merkabah.

1. Visualize and sense the energy of a mighty and incredibly beautiful Galactic Dragon stepping forward toward you. You can feel the energy around you begin to pulsate.
2. As you observe the dragon, they draw down a bright shimmering white light from high above you; this hovers as a bright ball of light a few feet above your head.
3. Your dragon draws the light down toward your galactic chakra and you feel all your energy centres respond.
4. Your own personal matrix becomes visible to you and the energy of it starts to form your very own Merkabah. You become aware of the energy flowing from you and to you. You feel your connection to the ancient wisdom of this, of your connection to Earth and to Gaia herself. As the energy of your Merkabah builds and grows feel for the gentle click as your energy essence and your Merkabah connect fully into place.

5. Feel your Merkabah encasing you in a ball of light. Allow yourself to become accustomed to this new high frequency energy as it settles into your system. In time it will enclose you in the full magnificence and completeness of who you are as a spiritual being.

6. Take some time asking for the dragons for help if you need it as the energy of the Merkabah moves through you.

7. Once you have completed what you need to do, sit with it, observe it and get a sense of it. How do you feel with it? Does it feel comfortable? Make any adjustments you need to; be guided by your own inner wisdom.

8. Open your eyes when you are ready. Check in with yourself and see how you feel.

The Merkabah ignites your inner wisdom, the place of intuition, and begins the journey of alignment to the universal energies. Sit with it and become familiar with it for it is you at your truest and purest self.

Welcome home!

DRAGON TIP

ALWAYS WORK WITH THE DRAGON ENERGIES WITH INTENTION.

CHAPTER

14

The Matrix and Light Grids

Now we come to the final chapter. It is here that all the other chapters get pulled together and I hope you can see the journey you have taken with me and your dragons as your guides.

This is the final piece of the puzzle for now, the dragons tell me. Although I am sure they will have much more to share with me in the coming years, just as they have over the last two decades. It is ever a progressing picture.

The Matrixes

When the dragons showed me the matrix (the Earth grids) two decades ago it looked to me like a beautiful and intricate spider's web. They explained that the Earth, galactic and crystal grids are all light strands. If you imagine a giant spider's web caught in bright sunshine on the crispest, coldest, frostiest winter morning you will see in your mind's eye what they showed me.

Where each strand crosses and intersects there is a dew drop. This is a crystallized light pattern that sends information in all directions from deep in the heavens to the deepest part of our Earth.

Everything within our world, the Universe and galaxies is connected via light, including galactic grids, Earth grids, crystal grids and our own light body. The light strands are wrapped around our Earth and connect with ancient sites such as Machu Picchu, the pyramids, stone circles, Glastonbury Tor, the Vatican and more. These invisible energies lines (they are not ley lines) connect the constellations in the skies (and some individual planets) and sacred sites, then to us as humans before diving down into the crystal grids deep below the Earth's surface.

These are the dragons' song lines. Through this light system of frequency we are able to connect energetically and completely to each other, our natural world, star beings, the dragons and more. We have been called by the dragons, the archangels, the Ascended Masters and the world's deities to work together to heal, clear and support the dragons' song lines.

Of course we have a choice. We have no need to heed their plea and we can carry on blindly and obliviously much in the same way we have for centuries. Although I do not feel we will as there are massive energy shifts taking place and we are aware of them. Throughout the year there are points when new vibrant bright and light energies enter our realm. We are invited to anchor and hold them as these portals of light bring in emerging awareness and great insights.

If we as humans want to be able to hold and channel the energies of the fifth to the ninth dimensions (and above) we need to be clear of all our earthly woes, fears and need for control. Our light bodies need to be in alignment with our soul's purpose as well as the Earth and the galactic light matrixes or more simply the crystal web of light.

Slowly we are gathering together as one, as the children of Earth. As individuals and groups do this work we become a tool and tuning device to lift the planet's energy. As more of us gather together, the greater chance there is of bringing balance to Earth, to reduce or even halt global warming, create world peace, tolerance and have unity over diversity. And that is simply the beginning.

DRAGON TALK

As ever when I am trying to wrap my head
around some of the more random stuff
the dragons drop in my lap, I turned
to them once more for clarity and I was
given this piece of information from the
Galactic Guardians.

*"We are Galactic Guardians. We are the
Guardians of the Light Matrix Grids.
Your planet's sacred and ancient sites
are the portal connection to us and you.
Activating them allows more people to
connect with us, but more importantly it is
about healing your planet."*

So as a Galactic Guardian you are the
protector of the light matrix and galactic
grid?

*"Not as such, we are here to guide you in
repairing and connecting the grids. You
have met the dragons that work with your
planet's sacred sites. Their work is to
take care of Earth's special sites. And you
in turn are being asked to work with the
Dragons of the Land to heal, repair and
clear these important places. They are a
part of your history, your ancestors and a
vital to the energy of your home. We take
care of the cosmic light grids."*

If I understand this right, the grids
are a series of light matrixes that line
up directly above the Earth's scared and
ancient sites.

"They line up, but not necessarily directly above. There is a connection between the star systems, in particular the rising and setting of the sun and the moon. This is well documented in your world.

"Stars and planets line up with your world's energy sites; we set this in motion eons ago. They act as a reminder that you are not alone in your Universe; there is great magic within your world, which you will recall."

Dragons of the Land

Earlier in the book you met the Dragons of the Land. Their work is to energetically keep clear any sites that they are the guardians of. They also have another role and that is to take care of the grids that run through them, the dragon song lines.

Matrix Healing Meditation

1. In your mind's eye see yourself within a sacred or ancient site. This can be anywhere in the world, such as Uluru, Machu Picchu, any of the stone circles or ancient groves, wherever you are drawn to. You may find yourself flitting about until you find the right spot for you energetically to do this work. Go with it, staying deep within your heart and your breath. Wherever you decide will be perfect and you will be guided by your higher knowing.

2. Once you have settled, feel your connection to the land there. Feel its ancientness. Feel yourself connect deeply with it, keeping your heart connection building.

3. On the periphery of your vision there is a glowing whiteish light. You turn to face it. As you watch, it builds to form a beautiful arch filled with illuminous light. You can feel its energy.

4. Once the arch has reached its peak, the Dragons of Light come pouring through it, flying toward you to form a large circle around you. They are iridescent, sparkling and shining and they are HUGE. You can feel their frequency – the ground beneath you vibrates slightly.

5. The dragons spread their wings, the tips touching and overlapping, and the energy increases further. As they do so the land around you lights up like a large spider web of light. This light is for the planet, for the whole of humanity. You feel drawn to gather the light under your feet. You can feel its energy.

6. The dragons show you the light grids around the Earth and how they connect to each other and the Earth's sacred sites. Some of the connecting lines are

damaged and out of shape, requiring clearing and rebalancing, and others are simply tired.

7. The Dragons of Light guide you in your next steps to release this light with the intent of healing, repairing and reconnecting the lines where appropriate. Follow your intuition and the dragons' guidance of what is required and what you need to do.

The greatest work we can do as individuals and collectively is to support the Dragons of the Land and the Galactic Dragons in keeping the dragon song lines clear. From this point, clear pure energy is passed around our planet into the crystal grids and the energy coming in from the celestial heavens can move and flow freely, guiding, enlightening and supporting our spiritual evolution. Together we will grow and blossom with our dragon guides.

DRAGON TIP

YOUR DRAGONS WILL ALWAYS GUIDE YOUR WAY AND YOUR WORK – SIMPLY ASK.

Closing Thoughts

As this book now draws to a close I hope you will understand why we have dragons to work with and why you too will discover your own uniqueness with them. Over the course of this mammoth task of writing and pulling together my own personal dragon experiences and channelled messages from the dragons themselves, I too have dived deep with the dragons and into myself.

When the dragons first introduced me to this work almost two decades ago, they thought we were ready to do the work. I am sure there were a few people around the world who were ready to do it but many more were not ready. We really were not anywhere near as spiritually adept or advanced as we or the dragons thought. It has taken almost 20 years for dragons to begin to teach and guide us as a collective.

As humans we are incredible and adaptable beings. Walking with our dragons beside us we can do anything we choose. Of course we have many other archetypes and energies to work with too. All of this is perfect and as it should be if we are to grow and thrive as a species and a planet.

In short, we can all work together to protect and begin to heal our lives, ourselves and our home – this beautiful and diverse floating rock called Earth. And now we have grown in number, it is time to share this work with you all.

Acknowledgements

My late mentor who I met when I was 17 told me "your greatest teachers will be your guides – make friends with them". Those words have never been truer than with our relationship and work with dragons.

There are so many who have supported me and my dragon work over the years. To each and every one of you, thank you.

My greatest gratitude has to be for my dragons, for bringing me Naz Ahsun, who literally walked into my life one Yule morning. Without her, you wouldn't have this book in your hands now.

I owe her and the Watkins team – in particular my editor Fiona Robertson for her belief, unwavering support and guidance through my initial manuscript attempts – a huge debt of gratitude for believing in a previously unknown me.

Their support of my work with the dragons has been quite honestly life changing.

Thank you!

It is also with gratitude to my friends and peers whom I have shared, worked and walked with. Their wisdom and insights have been invaluable. The dragons encourage us as humans to collaborate. So I learnt the extended chakra system and your own personal energy from my dear friend Ann Noble, a great spiritual teacher and dragon healing master. The section on colour was supported by another friend Andrea Webb. Her work is all about colour and crystals, and without her vast knowledge and insight I'd still probably be writing the colour notes!

A final thank you to the hundreds, if not thousands, of students and clients who have entrusted me with their personal dragon journeys.